S0-EQL-273

OFFICE
PLANNING
AND
DESIGN

OFFICE PLANNING AND DESIGN

OFFICE PLANNING AND DESIGN

MICHAEL SAPHIER Chairman SAPHIER, LERNER, SCHINDLER, INC.

McGRAW-HILL BOOK COMPANY
New York   San Francisco   Toronto   London   Sydney

OFFICE PLANNING AND DESIGN

Copyright © 1968 by McGraw-Hill, Inc. All Rights Reserved. Printed in the United States of America. No part of this publication may be reproduced, stored in a retrieval system, or transmitted, in any form or by any means, electronic, mechanical, photocopying, recording, or otherwise, without the prior written permission of the publisher. *Library of Congress Catalog Card Number 68-11237*

ISBN 07-054720-3

9 HDHD 80

TO RUTH *whose self-effacing aid and quiet comfort were given with unflagging devotion as the early days and nights of career building continued on into years without end.*

When the writing of this book was only an idea, I intended it to be a book that would touch briefly on the role of the planner and designer in formulating our environment, and then tell all about one branch of that effort: office space planning and design. But I really had no idea what "all about" actually meant.

As I thought about it, and when I began to work on it, I found myself as fascinated by the book as I am, and have been, with space planning itself. The book, I felt, had to be more than a textbook for the planner, interior designer, architect, or office manager; it had to be a worthy introduction to what will someday be a way of life for many of the design and architectural students who may read it.

AN INTRODUCTION TO A BOOK
...AND TO A WAY OF LIFE

The influence of environment on man, ignored completely in the dark ages of his past, was still given but little thought as the individual began to emerge from feudal obscurity. The unexpected change in the structure of our society took place much too rapidly to allow for any conscious planning for the future. The sudden growth of cities brought its own self-destructive inbreeding of poverty and crime and hate, all nurtured by an ignorance of, or an unwillingness to accept, the importance of planned environment.

But each day's unpredicted changes broadened man's horizons and brought him closer to the neighbor he had never known. As his world grew smaller and his knowledge of it greater, he began to appreciate man's interdependence. He learned that men walk together toward mutual understanding and that the peace that comes with understanding comes only when each carries his own inner dignity. Environment either adds to man's dignity or strips him of it. The plan and design of home, school, office, hospital, and museum are all parts of man's environment and from this was born the realization that space planning and design is rapidly becoming one of the more important sociological tools for man's improvement.

Planning and designing space is city planning as well as closet planning; it is the design of Lincoln Center for the Performing Arts or the East Falls Little Theatre; it is urban renewal and basement renovation. It is exciting because it is a career of exposure to living and of participation in this world of ours. The satisfaction of participation comes not merely from the contribution of an artistic talent, but also from the growth of that talent through the giving of one's time, energy, and intellect to understand and help in community activities and in the wholehearted sharing in humanity's search for fulfillment. Only this sharing, only this knowledge of man's needs, and only the knowledge that design must help meet these needs can make a good designer a great one. The problems are endless and the solutions limited only by our individual capacity for creativity. Our satisfactions become the multiple of our own enthusiasms.

Our automation marvels, our data-processing machines, are not the be-all and end-all of life. They are, in the final analysis, designed to be used by and for man. We may feel dehumanized by the series of numbers on a check that somewhere in the nether regions of the Federal Reserve System stand for us. We take comfort, however, in the knowledge that the check goes nowhere unless, by symbol or script, it has *our* signature on it.

Behind each check and charge account number, each magazine subscription and telephone number, each social security and savings bank number stands a man. No matter how complicated the technology of industry, or how advanced our systems of communication and transportation become, they are all planned by man and designed for his use. It is this participation in the role man plays in creating the future that makes the future ours to shape.

The work of space planning and design is done for people, and by people and with people. The designer just out of school, eager to prove his genius to a world waiting impatiently for his work, will have no work to show until he understands that what he is designing will be used by people only if it is honestly conceived for their use, only if they are comfortable using it, and only if it is practicable for them to use.

This is intended as a textbook, but not an orthodox one. It is a text on office planning specifically. It is not a book on architecture, but is a book for architects—and students of architecture. It is a book for practitioners and students of interior design, industrial design, interior decoration, office management, and business administration.

The problems with which it deals, the methods of getting to the heart of each problem, and the processes of arriving at solutions are basic to all planning and design. Whether the problem be planning a city, a building, or space within a building, the basic questions that must be answered are similar. The planner must study, understand, and design to suit the operational aims, the aesthetic goals, and the financial limitations of each problem—and he must follow his design through its building stage to its ultimate use.

In planning an office, the planner—be he architect or interior designer or office manager—must be as concerned with the layout of the mail room as he is with the layout of the president's office. The purpose of this book is to fill an informational gap and to deal in depth with the methods for unearthing and understanding the elements of office operation that are at the heart of each planning project.

It tells about the things that have to be done in space planning and design jobs and some of the ways in which they can be done. It lists usable standards, useful dimensions, and even some "do's and don'ts."

The drawings interspersed throughout the book have been included to help clarify specifics of the text. The photographs of completed installations illustrate the ways in which design can meet the challenges of functional requirements. A few show some of the basic methods used to save space. Others show how design details are used to solve problems that are due to the physical aspects of specific space. But all of them are design solutions created to solve functional problems. Informational checklists have been appended to the chapters throughout.

As planners and designers we have created, revised, rerevised, and used all these checklists in list, chart, and tabular form. We have seen the lists and charts and forms that other planners and designers have created and used. We have learned that though most contain similar information, each designer prefers to devise his own form and his own graphics. We are therefore not suggesting or showing any formats for these checklists. Instead the book concentrates on supplying the information that must be a part of each form.

Some will end up as simple lists, some as forms into which information will be written, while others may be forms on which appropriate boxes will be checked. Whatever the size or shape or design, it is important to remember that the form itself will not make for good planning and designing—that can come only from a thorough understanding and proper interpretation of the acquired information.

Each checklist is quite complete, and it contains all of the operational items required in your study. Unfortunately it is not possible to anticipate every direction into which checklist discussions can take you. Many are covered in the description of the use of each list, but the ingenuity of each planner and designer will lead him into his own paths of exploration.

The chapters are arranged to follow closely the logical procedural steps of space planning and design. In the interest of clarity of text, however, there is some deviation from the ideal step-by-step procedure. An itemized checklist has been appended to the last chapter of the book and it can be used when you review each project. Despite the lists, space planning and design is anything but a routine of precharted procedures. It is accomplished not only by checking off the things to be done, but also by doing them to accommodate the various problems and the various people whose very differences make each job an individual and exciting challenge. The lawyer whose clients are business corporations presents an image to clients that may be distinctly different from the image desired by the labor union lawyer. Each has a different philosophy, each has a different way of living, and each has an individual planning and design problem that must be studied, understood, and solved.

The first part of the book is concerned with the work of planning by design. The second part describes the organization and business aspects of a design company, and the job procedures necessary for the smooth operation of this kind of service business.

All the information contained herein aims to fulfill the original purpose of this book: to "tell all." If I have succeeded it is because of the wonderful cooperation from so many people, including Larry Lerner, Bud Schindler, and all of my other associates, who helped not only with the book itself but by making space planning and design so valid a career that a book about it became desirable. My thanks to my associates for their indulgence during the writing of this book and for their constructive criticism of its contents. My everlasting gratitude to the several secretaries in our office who devised their own Rosetta stone to make possible the deciphering of my handwriting. And, last, my wide-eyed admiration to my wife, who undangled my participles, united my infinitives, and clarified my obscurities.

Michael Saphier

CONTENTS

Introduction vii

YESTERDAY 1

PART I PLANNING BY DESIGN

CHAPTER I UNDERSTANDING 7

    I THE OPERATIONAL AIM 8
    II THE AESTHETIC GOALS 17
    III THE FINANCIAL LIMITATIONS 21

    CHECKLISTS
        A. Operational Requirements 23
        B. Departmental Questionnaire 33
        C. Inventory 34
        D. Design and Construction Requirements 36

CHAPTER II ANALYZING 41

    I THE AMOUNT OF SPACE REQUIRED 42
    II THE DIRECTION: RENT, BUILD, OR REMODEL 45
    III A PROGRAM FOR A NEW BUILDING 52

CHECKLISTS
    E. Tabulation Form 57
    F. Evaluation Report 58

CHAPTER III EXPLORING 63

    I SPACE USE 64
    II THE BUDGET 73
    III DESIGN 80

CHECKLISTS
    G. Space Study 86
    H. Work Letter 87

CHAPTER IV PREPARING 89

    I A DESIGN PRESENTATION 90
    II WORKING DRAWINGS 99
    III A PURCHASING PROGRAM 107

CHECKLISTS
    I. Design Presentation 110
    J. Working Drawings 111

CHAPTER V COORDINATING 115

    I THE BIDDING   116
    II THE BUILDING   119
    III THE MOVING   123

    CHECKLISTS
      K. The Move   126

PART II PLANNING FOR DESIGN

CHAPTER VI THE PRACTICE 159

    I OF OFFICE PRACTICE   160

CHAPTER VII ORGANIZING THE COMPANY 165

    I PERSONNEL   166
    II PROCEDURES   173
    III PHILOSOPHY   181

    CHECKLISTS
      L. Project Procedures   184

TOMORROW   187

Illustrations   189

Index   191

YESTERDAY

The very first office I can remember having seen was in an illustration for Charles Dickens's **A Christmas Carol.** Bob Cratchit, perched on a stool, throat wrapped in a threadbare muffler, sat at his high counting house table, making entries in a large ledger with a quill pen. The wind and snow crept through the cracks in the window, the tallow candle flickered, while the fireplace in the corner gave but an illusion of possible warmth. The only thing that can be said in faint praise of this office is that it did a wonderful job of reflecting true corporate image; it left no doubt concerning the character of Mr. Scrooge.

Business was uncomplicated and the advantages of planned environment unheard of in the days of Scrooge and Marley. But these days Bob Cratchit's stool is an upholstered swivel posture chair. The ledger sheet he examines has been printed by an IBM machine, and a formica-topped steel L-shaped desk has replaced his high, spindle-legged table. The flickering candle has given way to 100 footcandles of evenly distributed light at desk level. The sealed windows will never let in snow or wind, and the air conditioning that has sealed them has also done away with the need for a fireplace.

The new concepts in office-building construction and the technical

2 Office Planning and Design

advances in such fields as lighting and air conditioning came into use in the late 1940s, when our industries were able to turn again to peacetime pursuits. Interior planning faced many new problems, not the least of which was the problem of coping with the huge expanse of floor space made possible in modern buildings.

Many other factors added to the complications of renting (or building), planning, and designing business space. Business itself became more sophisticated. Administrative, sales, and distributive functions assumed more and more importance as, little by little, the white-collar workers outnumbered the blue. Planning for the new electric and electronic equipment and the even newer ways in which they could be used took on greater, more urgent significance. The human factor, the need for reflecting the company and its people through environment, became a vital planning consideration. Practical and emotional complexities dictated the need for major changes in the utilization of office space.

To compound the problem for the space user, building costs increased, rents increased, and the cost of all other services peripheral to space use were similarly escalated. Each square foot of space cost so much to rent, furnish, and maintain that its planning and design could no longer be left in the hands of the well-meaning company vice-president, office manager, or sales manager, who, in the days prior to the 1940s, handled 99 percent of company moves.

Even though it was a relatively simple task in those days, it was poorly done. Space was wasted through a lack of understanding of the overall company problems. Communications and work flow suffered from the same lack. Time, money, and comfort were sacrificed because of the amateur space planner's inability to plan creatively or to take advantage of the technical improvements available to him.

In the 1930s a handful of designers involved in one way or another with designing for industry became interested in the way business used its office space. Anticipating the inevitable economic growth of the country and the coming building boom, they began preparing for their own place in this program by expanding their knowledge of business operations, of the construction industry, and of interior design. Most important of all, they learned how to blend the essential ingredients of each of these efforts into a new industry—space planning and design.

Today the services of the space planner and designer are called upon by corporations, institutions, and government agencies, as well as realtors, builders, and architects. The space planner's work during the past thirty years has involved him in the study of millions of square feet of office space. He has had to analyze occupied space, new space into which his client was moving, and space which would be built for his client. He has been concerned with the amount of space to be used, the size and shape of the building in which it was to be used, and, most important, the validity of erecting that building or renting space in it.

From this overwhelming exposure to industry a new set of procedures has evolved in techniques of planning and designing geared to supply the maximum utilization of interior work space, while at the same time creating a working environment in which each individual could function with individual dignity and to the fullest of his productive capacity.

PART I PLANNING BY DESIGN

CHAPTER I UNDERSTANDING

There are no meaningful answers without a thorough understanding of the problem. Trite as this statement may be, it has such validity that it must be repeated again and again until it becomes a way of life for the designer. Probing the problem—searching out all possible approaches to an answer—is the challenge and the reward for the man who is a designer because he has no choice: he must be a designer!

It makes no difference how simple or complex the problem. The answer is good only if it is arrived at honestly. No clever shortcuts, no surface coatings, can withstand the scrutiny of time or should withstand one's own analytical self-criticism.

In office planning and design, whether the problem is concerned with placing five people where four now sit or with planning a building for five hundred people, whether with the redesign of a vice-president's office or with the design of the executive complex of a major industrial corporation, the same questions must be asked. The extent of the questioning, the details into which it delves, may vary, but the purpose is the same: to understand as much as possible about the problem in order to make sure that the answer is a valid one. ■

SECTION I UNDERSTANDING THE OPERATIONAL AIM

The information gathered in order to understand the operational aims of the client serves several purposes, of which two, of major importance, are of interest in this section. From these **operational requirements** you must be able, first, to translate the client's needs into a tabulation of the amount of space necessary to house his company, and, second, to translate the two dimensions of his ideal organizational chart into the three dimensions of office space.

Since the solutions to these problems come from the answers to the questions that are asked, it is vital not only that you ask the right questions but also that you develop a sensitivity to the answers. You must learn to judge whether each question is being answered objectively in the best interest of the client's company or whether it is dealt with subjectively for the self-aggrandizement of the person questioned.

Depending upon the size or the needs of the client, the questions concerning his requirements will be put to one or more people. If the client company is a large one and the problem involves extensive relocation, it would be wise for the client to appoint one person (or a small committee capable of speaking as one person) to answer those questions and to act as liaison between client and planner in validating the answers. Since this liaison task must be referred to quite often in this book, the client's representative shall hereafter be designated as "management."

It is from management, then, that you get your first exposure to the client's operational requirements, and in doing so you will come face to face with the first of many **checklists**. (These lists will be found at the end of each chapter.) Each of these lists will play some part in each job to be done. It is, therefore, important that these checklists be not only scrupulously utilized, but expanded as use dictates more items to be checked. Of course, as planner and designer you will do your best to be so thoroughly familiar with the checklists that you will need to refer to them only often enough to make sure you have missed nothing. You will find that by paying too close attention to the prepared checklist, by rigidly adhering to the printed page and its check boxes, you are losing contact with the person questioned and failing to get him personally involved in the questioning. The checklist should be a springboard for management, giving the one you are questioning an opportunity to talk freely about any and all aspects of his operation. Remember, you are there to learn all you

Understanding the Operational Aim

can about the client's business. This can be done only when you can get him to talk about it. When you are talking, you are merely repeating things you already know; when you listen, you may learn something you did not know.

Before starting the question-and-answer session with management, there are some documents which, if available, would be of help in the progress of the job. A list of these documents should be given to management in advance of the requirement-taking meeting so that, if possible, they can be made available to you at the meeting. It would in fact be wise also to brief management in advance and in as much detail as possible concerning the kinds of questions you will be asking. There is nothing wrong with giving him a copy of **Checklist A—Operational Requirements** (page 23) prior to your meeting. Such procedure can only make for shorter, more informative sessions.

One document that can be of great help is the **plan** (or **plans**) of the space now being occupied by the client. The more detailed these plans are in their delineation of private offices, departments, personnel locations, furniture, equipment, etc., the more help they will be in your understanding of the existing operation. If available plans are not up to date but can be made so without too much work, it would be advisable for the planner to spend the time necessary to bring them up to date. They can later be used as a check on things you will have seen during your tour of the space.

The next document that could be of help is the client's table of organization or **organization chart.** Since the ideal office layout is an extension into three dimensions of this chart, the help that it can be is obvious. The more detailed the chart, the better. It should show intradepartmental relationships, interdepartmental relationships, the relationships of departments to executives and to service arms, and any other organization relationships that can be charted. If a chart does not exist (and not many companies have one), it is going to be made one way or another. In a simple job of planning, the experienced planner and designer will make the chart as he prepares the **space study;** in fact, the space study will be the chart. (The space study and its relationship to the organization chart will be fully described in Chapter III. For the moment understand it as the first basic plan that will be made to show how the client's organization will fit into a specific area.) In studying more complicated business operations, the planner may find it worthwhile to rough out an organization chart before he begins the space study. For the beginner, the chart will certainly be of great help in his approach to the actual study.

Another document that must be made available to the planner and designer in one form or another is the **personnel list.** This should be as detailed as possible, with personnel listed by departments and in job categories. The list not only will serve as a check on the number of people employed, but should give you some understanding of the work each does.

Last are the documents that can give background information on the company. This kind of material contains nothing of importance to the basic details of the job, but can add considerably to your knowledge of the client and your overall knowledge of his operation. Within this category of documents are such things as **financial statements** in which corporate aims are set forth, **company brochures, house organs,** and **catalogs.** When a client has no such documents, the background information that will be helpful to you will have to be obtained later from interviews. The most important information, however, will come from your review with management of Checklist A—Operational Requirements. This checklist, and an explanation for its use, can be found on page 23. The answers you get from the client in your review of the checklist will start you on your way toward understanding the full scope of the problem ahead.

One thing that should be stressed at this point is the importance of taking copious notes covering everything that is said. There will be many meetings at which many decisions will be made. Meetings may last an hour, four hours, or two days. A tremendous amount of information will be gathered and innumerable decisions will be made—more information and more decisions, in fact, than anyone can possibly remember. You may start, confidently feeling that you will remember everything, but it doesn't take long to find out that the man to whom you are talking may change his mind about a single question three or four times during the course of the interview. Since he said "yes' three times and "no" four times to the same question, you will be hard pressed to remember which is the proper answer unless it is written down. This involvement in a myriad of details is so much a part of each plan and design job that the taking of notes at all meetings and during all telephone conversations with the client is essential.

Understanding the Operational Aim 11

How should these records or **minutes of meetings** be taken? They can be taken in any of several ways: by tape recording, by a stenographer, or by your own handwritten notes. Tape recording seems to have disadvantages that outweigh its advantages. The recorder tends to make many people self-conscious, and so prevents those who feel finality in the taped word from communicating easily. Other people, when interviewed, are too wordy for taped recordings, and the job of sifting the important conversation from the tape can be tedious, time-consuming, and often unproductive. When the taped word is transcribed by a secretary, the draft must be edited and retyped to be of value and that, too, is a time-consuming and costly process.

The second way of taking minutes, by having a secretary present to take notes in shorthand, is cumbersome because the secretary must take down every word of conversation without the ability to be discriminating. With this process, as with the tape recorder, too much material must be typed, edited, and retyped.

Experience has shown that the best results come from writing your own notes. This gives you the opportunity to listen, participate, write, and, in writing, remember better.

These minutes not only provide you with an understanding of the job ahead but they are the outlines of the job. In addition, they must perform another very vital function as a check on the validity of what was said to you. Minutes of every meeting, every telephone conversation in which a decision is made, and every client change made on the job should be noted, dictated, typed, and sent to the client for his review and approval or change. Each job of planning and design must have its complete file of minutes of meetings. Through this double check on what has been said and on the interpretation of its meaning, many costly errors of both omission and commission can be avoided.

Minutes afford the client a second, more critical look at his own first and sometimes hastily made decisions. Minutes helped one client realize that because the company's export division was housed at a different location from the rest of the company, he had forgotten to include it.

Minutes also help pinpoint the source of information. After one client had moved into new space, one of the vice-presidents complained that his department had been placed farther away from him than he desired it to be. It was, in fact, on another floor. An examination of the minutes revealed that the decision had been made at the very beginning of the job by the same vice-president who now objected to the placement.

These minutes can be presented as letters to the client, job memorandums, or reports on a specially designed form. This would be a matter of personal planner and designer preference. It will be up to management to decide how many copies of these minutes he would like to have and how they should be distributed within his company.

The minutes of meetings also play an important part in the production of the plans and designs for the client job. This role will be described later in the discussion of the organization of a design company and its procedures.

Immediately after completing the review of Checklist A—Operational Requirements, you should go on an **inspection tour** of the company premises to see the offices, departments, and service arms that have just been described. Ideally this tour should be conducted by the same man or men who supplied the answers to the checklist questions. The tour should be all-inclusive, and no part of the operation should be missed. Depending upon your prior familiarity with the type of business in which this particular client is engaged, it may or may not be necessary to augment the tour by spending several hours or several days in all or some of the client's departments. In order to analyze your client's needs thoroughly, it is necessary that you know exactly how the company functions and what the duties are of each person in the company. To learn more about the interrelationship of some of the client's departments you may, for example, want to follow a purchase order from its arrival in the morning mail through the processes of order filling, accounting, billing, and filing. You may want to attend a sales meeting to help determine the kind of physical facilities that would best contribute to the smooth running of such meetings. You may want to watch a typist at work in order to provide her with a **work station** that will meet all her requirements for forms, stationery, and filing facilities.

Management will, of course, arrange for this kind of job study, just as it will have arranged for your tour. But it will be up to you to advise management of the necessity and methods for preparing his personnel for their exposure to you. The sight of a stranger taking more than a casual tour of the premises, a stranger who asks questions, takes notes, and observes office activity for hours at a time, always makes company personnel uneasy. Each man begins to worry about his boss, his company's solvency, or his job. So it is wise for management to take certain steps prior to the start of a tour, advising all personnel that a tour will be made and why it will be made. In addition, the memo or letter carrying this advice, should state the advantages that the retained consultant will eventually bring to the company and to the working conditions of each individual. The letter should mention the fact that the consultant and his staff will visit the office on many occasions to observe activity and to take inventory of all furniture and equipment.

Checklist A—Operational Requirements, the tour, **Checklist B—Departmental Questionnaire**, and the **inventory taking**, are all checks on each other as well as ways of gathering additional information about the client. While on tour it is always a good idea to check out the number of people in each department (counting heads can be quickly done), the number of files within each department, if there is a concentration of more than just a few, as well as any other equipment that occupies floor space, such as safes or storage cabinets. A more detailed count of people and equipment will be made when the inventory is taken and when you check the personnel list. However, familiarity with the individual department's problems, gained through tour exposure, will help in your understanding of the total problem and in arriving at the eventual solutions to those problems. For example, knowledge of the existence of a storage cabinet within a department can lead to the use of space-saving ideas that could do away with that cabinet entirely. Files that have for years been accepted as necessary could, when it is pointed out that they occupy expensive floor space, either disappear partially or entirely, or be relegated to a central file room.

During the tour do not hesitate to ask questions, even though you may repeat these questions later in your interviews. The checking and rechecking of information and opinion can only lead to the clarification of each.

To augment the information gathered in discussing the operational requirements, and in taking a tour of the premises in order to observe the organization at work, you must now become thoroughly familiar with the work and interrelationship of each department or division or other unit of organization that exists in the client company.

Becoming familiar with a department's work means **interviewing** and questioning the department head or anyone else management designates to supply the answers for which you are looking.

At times the manner in which management designates the persons to be interviewed and the manner in which the interview is to take place can be rather startling to even the most experienced planner and designer. For example, the president of a rather large company publishing trade magazines issued instructions that were strange indeed. The checklist of operational requirements was reviewed with him, and he was told of the designer's desire to interview his department heads. On the first page of a legal-size pad he wrote the name of each of his departments and the name of the man in charge. He then gave the pad to his designer with instructions to "interview each one of these men and find out what each wants or thinks he wants in the way of facilities for his department in our new offices. Find out how many people he needs, the kind of equipment he wants, and the percentage of expansion he thinks should be provided. Write down all the answers on this pad. When you come back we will tear up the pad and I will tell you what to give them." This approach, fortunately, is extremely unusual. After the interviews he did not tear up the pad, but he did compare the things the department heads had asked for with those he wanted to give them. It was quite obvious from this comparison that there were several areas of his own business about which the president knew nothing. And rightly so, because in every business of any size management cannot possibly know all of the details of the procedures that must be taken on by department heads.

The kinds of questions you ask department heads can vary somewhat according to the specifics of each job. It will be up to you to edit them by eliminating unnecessary questions from Checklist B—Departmental Questionnaire, as well as by adding more pertinent ones. On page 33 there is an example of a typical departmental questionnaire, along with explanations for its use. It covers such questions as the work the department does, its relationship with other departments, and its anticipated expansion by personnel and by equipment. In this area of questioning it is of utmost importance that you learn to appraise the validity of the answers you get.

Historically, department heads will, unchallenged, ask for more space than the entire company is planning to build or rent. Not that each is being selfish, but simply because, as a good department head, he is convinced that his department is the most important in the company.

In planning the space for a building that was to be built for a TV and radio station, one of the men interviewed was the business manager. During the course of the interview he asked for a small office for his own use, with room in an area outside his office for ten desks, files, storage for forms, and some miscellaneous equipment. The tour through his small department had revealed only five desks in the open area. You just can't challenge a man with "Why do you need ten desks?" without having him resent your interference. It is very important that everybody in the company be left with the correct idea that you are there to help, not to hinder, so the interviewer, in his questioning, quietly brought out the fact that the department is responsible for sending out bills to sponsors of the commercial time sold by the station, that all of the available time was sold, that there would never be more bills going out monthly than were now going out, and that the present staff was adequate for the task without doing any overtime work. It was then apparent to the business manager as well as the interviewer that, since no additional help was really needed, only five desks were required for the department. Since five additional desks and the equipment that would go with them would have taken up about 500 square feet of space, the cost of the space, at $20 per construction foot, would have been $10,000. Add to this sum the cost of the furniture and equipment and the cost of maintaining and cleaning both the furniture and the 500 square feet of space, and it becomes rather obvious that a considerable sum of money was saved by asking the right questions and validating the answers.

This is a perfect story to illustrate the necessity for questioning all unsubstantiated demands. It is difficult to imagine that any such pat situation will ever come up again. But when the head of the copy department in an advertising agency tells you that his twenty-man department will need two more people by next year, or when the head of a sales department of a paper company tells you that his plans call for doubling his division's sales in the next ten years, and that he will need thirty people instead of fifteen, you will be hard pressed to challenge either statement, no matter how adroit your questioning.

This is where your minutes of meetings are put to good use. All of the

16   *Planning by Design*

information gathered in the use of Checklist A—Operational Requirements and Checklist B—Departmental Questionnaire should be submitted to management for review, correction, and addition before you can continue in your examination of the overall problem. Management of the advertising agency could now tell you that plans to obtain two more large clients are far enough advanced to make it mandatory that the copy department have not two, but six more people by next year. Management of the paper company, on the other hand, could inform you that, unknown to the sales department head, the production of the particular paper handled by his division is being curtailed, so that the department will need eight people, not thirty.

One way or the other, it is vital that all answers to all questions be thoroughly scrutinized before they are translated into too many or too few square feet. It is not always possible to provide properly for the future. Too often it is necessary to use a rather cloudy crystal ball. But both planner and management will be remiss in their duties if they fail to recognize, understand, and interpret the predictable areas of operational study. It is just as wrong to build or rent too much space as it is to build or rent too little.

Before, during, or after the department-head interview a complete inventory of all furniture and equipment must be taken. The order is unimportant and may depend upon the manpower available to the planner and designer. **Checklist C—Inventory** and suggestions for its use are described on page 34. The inventory will serve many useful purposes. This list of all furniture and equipment, showing size, type, and condition, will give you an opportunity to appraise the adequacy of the equipment for the job to be done. Is the rolltop desk efficient for the bookkeeper or should it be replaced with an L-shaped desk, the component parts of which are so designed as to house his files and ledgers without using a storage cabinet or a file cabinet that occupies space?

The inventory form should have, in addition to the list of existing furniture and equipment, columns for furniture and equipment required for expansion purposes. By providing columns for the assignment of square feet to the furniture and equipment in each list, you can use the inventory form for tabulating the total footage required for your client's use.

The inventory will serve you further when you arrive at the point of

Understanding the Aesthetic Goals

preparing your **furniture plan.** If you have included on it information covering the electrical equipment, typewriters, and calculators being used by each person, as well as the individual's need for telephone equipment, the inventory will be of help in the preparation of the furniture, **telephone,** and **electrical plans.**

Finally, the inventory will aid you to prepare and check the client's **purchasing program,** which will be discussed in Chapter IV. The inventory will be a much-used document, and all inventory information must be gathered conscientiously, accurately, and in detail, with all its eventual uses kept constantly in mind during its preparation.

SECTION II UNDERSTANDING THE AESTHETIC GOALS

From the answers gathered in this second part of the effort to understand the problem will come the information and the inspiration for the design of the client's space—the face that he will present to his public, the image of his company, and the environment within which he and his people will spend so many of their waking hours. Just as it was necessary to interpret carefully the answers you received when you took the operational requirements, so is it equally important to acquire a sensitivity toward understanding the discussions you will have about the aesthetic goals of the client. And they will be discussions that you will be having, rather than question-and-answer periods—discussions that will be informative or not, depending a little on the client's ability to talk taste, design, and aesthetics, and a great deal on your ability to get him to talk.

The process of getting him to talk takes place at a **design meeting** or meetings, which will be described here and in Section III of this chapter as well. This design meeting must serve not only to help you understand the aesthetic goals, but also to set up the **budget** limitations to your design effort.

As a rule, the client representatives at the design meeting are not the people concerned with operational aspects of the problem. Usually the design meetings are attended by the president of the company and any other executives dealing with the company's public. The liaison management should, of course, be present. In addition, sales executives, advertising executives, and even public relations consultants are often invited to participate.

However, far more is accomplished at those meetings at which only one or two people are present. Historically discussions on philosophy of design bring forth many varied opinions, and management is often embarrassed by a lack of unanimity toward design approach among its own people.

But whether the discussion be with one person or twelve, you must still leave the meeting with a clear-cut idea of the direction design must take. And the client should be just as clear about what to expect from you! Understand that, as a rule, most clients will have great difficulty in verbalizing about design at the beginning of a design meeting. It will be up to you to do your utmost to help him express his ideas and lead him into new ideas if his do not adequately or properly reflect the company he heads. Since his next exposure to design will be when you are ready to make your design presentation, he had best be prepared for the things you will show him, and the best preparation is clear understanding of the directions and decisions made when design was first discussed.

Actually, there are only three basic questions that are to be discussed in that part of the design meeting concerned with aesthetics: **theme, period,** and **color,** and sometimes the first and second meld into one.

Theme, idea, image—whatever it is called—is the picture of the company as the client envisions it, as you help create and interpret it, and as the public is to see it.

- The book publisher who wants a "scholarly" look
- The chemical company wanting a "worldwide" look
- The charity organization that asks for "genteel poverty" as its public picture

These are the faces of your clients. These are the faces your client must describe to you.

And herein is the underlying problem of the design meeting—getting the client to articulate about his company's image. Don't for one moment think that his lack of ability to talk image is an indication of either lack of interest or lack of knowledge. The designer who believes that design talk is his own private domain and design itself his own inscrutable, ritualistic magic does his client an injustice and underestimates the power of design

Understanding the Aesthetic Goals

itself. Remember, if your client wasn't thoroughly aware of the need for design and the tangible and intangible benefits to be derived from it, he would not be at the design meeting in the first place.

The client's problem—and it is certainly not the problem of all clients—is that he is not used to talking design in his day-to-day conversation. It is up to you to make him feel at ease by first talking about the things that are familiar to him—the familiar things that will lead both of you directly to the whole design subject.

Sometimes the best way to do this is to review what you have learned about the company and its business goals and then have the client talk on from there. At other times it will be well to ask the client to talk about what his company has done and what he expects it to do. Either way, you must eventually get back to the discussion of how these goals can best be reflected through design.

The book publisher who asked for the "scholarly" look actually wanted to give the visitor the idea that he was entering a library. He wanted an archival atmosphere of hushed reverence for books to prevail in his offices. To accomplish this it was necessary to physically separate the sales and production part of his business from the editorial wing.

The chemical company that wanted a "worldwide" look was motivated by sales aims. The products the company sold were made up of raw materials purchased all over the world, and they wanted their buyers, who came from all over the world, to know this. This was not a preconceived theme but one, rather, that developed during conversation about the company products.

The "genteel poverty" desired by the charity organization client came from a direct demand to avoid giving the impression that contributed funds had paid for self-aggrandizement or necessary "creature comforts."

But not all your clients are going to fall into such neat descriptive slots. In fact, in most cases you are going to have to find your own way to present the client's image.

Very often, in his desire to draw out the client in design discussions, the designer will verbalize design ideas. One word of caution through repetition of something said before: listening, rather than talking, should be the rule in design meetings. Most certainly you should not, in your desire to show what a clever designer you are, talk about ways in which you might approach the design problem. Chances are that you will change your mind many times before you are ready to present your final design to the client who, because of something you said, may be anticipating something completely different. Once, in a careless moment at a design meeting, a curved wall was mentioned as a possible design solution to a reception-room problem. Several weeks later a straight-wall solution, which happened to have been the proper one, was rejected by the client, who had been intrigued by the idea of a curved wall and insisted upon having it.

At times the search for a theme may end in finding the key in practical merchandising solutions. Observation of the manner in which an overseas airline company sold its tickets in a street-level store led to a complete change in ticket handling and, in turn, to radical changes in the design of such facilities. Desks were substituted for counters, comfortable chairs replaced stools, and relaxed ease took over in place of cold, impersonal efficiency. All this was done because research recorded that nine out of ten customers were women excited about their European trip and anxious to be treated as though the airline was just as excited about it.

Discussion and observation, on the other hand, may reveal nothing distinctive, nothing adaptable to visual presentation except for such one-word descriptions as "stolidity," "contemporary," and "progressive," all of which lap over into the second basic question concerning period.

Is the client's business best reflected by contemporary design or do you haunt the antique shops to find a number of rolltop desks, high stools, and green eyeshades? Sometimes the theme dictates the period; sometimes the answer comes from further probing.

Taking a client on a tour of completed jobs, in order to get his reaction to various design approaches, is of great help when a client is completely unable to talk design.

This subject is covered again under Exploring Design (page 80). At this first meeting on design whatever guiding you do must be done as a basic educational process. The client must be made to understand how unorthodox it is to draw upon the periods of the past for the design of offices into which he is moving in the present, and which themselves are located in buildings attempting to reflect the future. It is equally curious if he, the client, expects Chippendale to properly reflect his electronic instrument manufacturing company.

Understanding the Financial Limitations

The one thing you must not do, if yours is to be honest design, is to attempt to guide your client into areas in which you feel comfortable without thought to his basic problem of image projecting. This does not mean that you give the client his blue bathroom because he asked for it. Neither do you give him a green one because all the bathrooms you have done have been green. It is vitally important to your growth as designers that you search constantly for better solutions, rather than create your own design clichés because of convenience or laziness.

The third basic question to be answered concerns color. It is generally not a difficult question because people tend to be quite definite about colors they like or dislike, and have no hesitation in telling about these preferences.

Trouble can come when the client insists that he has neither strong color likes nor dislikes. For one client with no color preferences (he said), drawings were prepared of his office with blue as the predominant color. His reaction was violent: "Can't stand blue and never could—in anything—change it!" So the whole design process started over again, despite the fact that the speech was made by a blue-eyed man wearing a blue suit, blue tie, blue shirt, and blue socks.

Except for an expression of color preference or color dislike, discussions on color with the client will usually bring forth little information. How we use color to aid in our image creating will be covered in Chapter III (Exploring Design) and Chapter IV (Preparing a Design Presentation).

SECTION III UNDERSTANDING THE FINANCIAL LIMITATIONS

Money seems to be the one thing that most designers prefer not to talk about. Like it or not, however, it is a subject that absolutely cannot be ignored. It must be faced many times during the course of a job, and any lack of desire to face it is not only thoroughly unrealistic but can be disastrous as well. It must be faced at the beginning so that all of your design effort is done without costing any more than the dollars allotted you by the client. It must be faced during the course of the job so that the cost of client extras or client changes is completely understood before either is authorized. And it must be faced at the end of the job so that the client is thoroughly aware of the fact that you have not only met his operational requirements and his aesthetic aims, but his budgetary limitations as well. Failure to meet any one of these can result only in an unhappy client, and this was certainly not your goal when you started the job.

Determining the budget limitations not only provides you with the information about the number of dollars you may spend, but defines the areas in which these dollars are to be spent.

Whether the client tells you how much money he has allocated for the job or whether he asks you to tell him how much the work should cost, it is your responsibility to see that his money is spent wisely and effectively.

If he has a given amount budgeted, you must help decide where it can be spent most tellingly. If you are to determine the dollars he needs, you must help appraise his requests. In either event your first job is to go through **Checklist D—Design and Construction Requirements,** and get answers to each of the questions it contains. The list and an explanation for its use follow at the end of this chapter on page 36. From the answers obtained, you will later prepare the budget of costs involved in the job and the bill of particulars that will aid in the preparation of the **workletter** portion of a lease (Chapter II).

The budget will also provide you with your guide to design—the framework of dollars within which all your design effort must stay.

The infinite number of details involved in each planning and design job makes budgeting a necessity. If you were not to budget a job before designing and drafting, you would listen to your client describe the things he thinks he wants, prepare perspective renderings and design details, and get his enthusiastic approval, which would quickly turn to disapproval of both design and designer when bids to do the work came in at prices far beyond what he thought he might have to spend. Budgeting gives the client the opportunity to know just what his costs might be before seeing any drawings. It also gives him the opportunity to lower or raise those costs by editing his requirements prior to your preparing any drawings.

In the course of your questioning, the client may ask for a color TV for the president's office and a refrigerator-bar in the conference room. By placing a dollar value on these requests before doing any design work

Checklist A   23
Operational
Requirements

or any detail drawing, you can come back to the client and show him what the things he has asked for will cost. The color TV may change to black-and-white (or be eliminated entirely), while the refrigerator-bar becomes the ice cubes in the general office water cooler.

As you get more and more familiar with the discussion of design and the budgets that are prepared after those discussions, you will begin to gain a sensitivity to these needs and an understanding of the dollars that may be involved even before you start work on the budget. When you feel secure about your ability to guess at the overall cost of a job with a fair degree of accuracy, it will help prepare the client for the budget you will present later if you let him know that the job he is talking about could cost approximately x to y dollars.

The budget will also provide the client with the opportunity to analyze all aspects of a move. He may, for instance, feel that new furniture in a general office might call for an expenditure he can ill afford. An insurance company had fifty people in its accounting department, all working at overly large, old desks that the company had no intention of replacing. A new L-shaped desk provided the same work surface, but saved 10 square feet per person. This meant a saving of 500 square feet of space at a rental of $6 per square foot per year. Over a twenty-year lease this represented a savings of $60,000. Management decided on new desks. But even if new desks had not been purchased the budget gave management the opportunity to make the decision.

Chapter III will cover the methods of budgeting and the importance of accuracy in pricing all the work and materials that go to make up a job. You must first be concerned, however, with making certain that all the things that have to be done, and all the things that have to be purchased, are listed for budgeting.

CHECKLIST A OPERATIONAL REQUIREMENTS

The order in which the items on the list are discussed is unimportant. The client may have his own way of describing his operation, and it would be wise to proceed in any way calculated to make him more comfortable. It is up to you to see that all items are covered. You will find that the client who wants to be guided will prefer the sequence of this list because it most closely resembles a "walk" through his own space.

When you list the client's requirements it would be well to start off by assigning an **identification number** to each person, department, conference room, etc. This number, if properly carried on all documents, will be a very important tool in checking inventories, budgets, space studies, working drawings, moving plans, etc. The numbering system should be kept as simple as the size of the project allows.

Reception Room

Number of seats
Receptionist
Display

How many people gather in the reception room at one time for whom seating must be provided? If traffic is extremely heavy, as it would be in the case of an advertising agency that does its own casting for TV commercials, would it then be wise to have two different kinds of reception areas: one for executive reception and the other as a working reception area? Are there any other operational considerations that could possibly indicate the need for more than one reception room?

Is the receptionist to be only that? Will she sit in the reception room and, if so, will she have any other duties such as typing or card-index filing, or any other duties requiring special furniture or equipment? Will the receptionist also run the switchboard or monitor board? If so, should she be in an enclosed area for call-handling privacy? If the receptionist does not run the switchboard, could the switchboard operator be the relief receptionist by being placed next to the reception room and available behind a sliding panel? Could the receptionist be one of the personnel in the general office, available behind glass, sliding panel, or low railing?

Is there a requirement for display of any kind that would occupy floor space? Is there need for literature to be displayed or distributed? Are there any operational requirements calling for personnel traffic control to various departments from the reception room? Are there any other factors, including corporate importance, that could affect the size of the reception room?

Checklist A 25
Operational
Requirements

Executive Area

Private offices
Secretaries
Conference or board rooms, dining areas
Private toilets
Kitchens or pantries

You must know the names and titles of the executives requiring private offices within the executive area. You must know whether or not there is any organizational protocol that would dictate the relative sizes of each office within this area, or any other area for that matter. You must know whether the size of each office would be affected by any equipment that must be housed in it, as well as by any operational use to which it must be put. Will any of these rooms be used for conferences or for meetings that require more than ordinary seating? Are there any closet or storage problems to be met within any of the offices that would affect its size? What is the desirable operational adjacency of one executive to another? Is there need for any executive to be near his department?

Is there a need to provide extra offices for VIP visitors? Should any offices be set up for future executives, and will these rooms for expansion require that other facilities also be provided, such as secretaries?

Which of the executives have secretaries? How many for each? Should the secretaries be in or outside the executive offices? If outside, can they share an executive corridor, should they have private offices of their own, or can two share an office between the private offices of the executives for whom they work? Should the secretary's office be the entrance to the executive's office? Should any executive have an inner reception area monitored by his secretary? Would it be desirable that the executive wing have an inner area where more important callers may be received?

You should know whether or not there is need for a conference room or boardroom in the executive area and how many people it must accommodate for table seating and auditorium seating. Is any purpose served by providing two rooms separated by a folding wall that can be opened to make one large room of the two? Is there need for projection equipment? If so, are the needs great enough to warrant a projection room? Is there need for corkboard, chalkboard, display panels of any kind, ledge for display boards, etc.? Will any dining take place here or elsewhere in the executive wing, and what kind of facilities will be required to provide for this dining: full kitchen or warming pantry? Are there any bar facilities desired? Is there a need for a telephone room next to the conference room, so that meetings are not disturbed when one of the people at the meeting has to take or make a call?

Is there a need, within the executive area, for any private toilets, showers, sinks, etc.? Should they be for general executive use, assigned to any particular executive, or assigned for conference room use?

Departments
  Private offices
  Semiprivate offices
  Secretaries
  Open areas—personnel
  Open areas—equipment
  Special requirements

(If department heads are to be interviewed, the items in this part of the checklist can be skimmed over once lightly. They will be discussed in more detail at a later meeting with the department head, when you will use the questionnaire of Checklist B on page 33.)

What are the names of each department, division, or any other unit component of the company? What are the interrelationships of the departments and what is the desirability for their adjacency? Do any departments have a large amount of traffic from the outside requiring closer proximity to the reception area?

What are the names and titles of any personnel within departments for whom private offices are to be provided? (Concerning these private offices the same questions can be asked that were asked about private offices in the executive area.)

Is there a need within the department for semiprivate offices housing two or more people?

What are the secretarial needs for the departments? Are the secretaries to be adjacent to the people for whom they work or should they be in a secretarial pool?

How many people are there in each open area of each department?

Checklist A
Operational
Requirements

Do they all do the same kind of work? Should they be physically divided into work units? Is there any other working relationship of personnel within the department, i.e., any people who work together and who should, therefore, be placed close to each other?

What provision should be made for expansion in each department and in what categories of work effort will expansion take place? How many additional private or semiprivate offices should be anticipated in each department?

What equipment does each use: desks, tables, tub files, etc.? Is there a need for any special equipment that occupies floor space? Is there a heavy concentration of files and are any files assigned to specific personnel?

Are there special requirements to meet a specific department's operational needs such as vault space, storage space, and departmental conference rooms? These special-purpose areas will be discussed later in this checklist so that company needs, common to all departments, will be thoroughly covered. When checking the list the planner can again make certain that any specific department needs for these facilities will be considered.

Special-purpose Offices

Many companies will have to provide offices for the office manager, the personnel manager, the chief of maintenance, etc. These offices are usually independent of any particular department. You will have to know what each man does, what space he needs for any staff he may have, what he requires in his office, and what he may need to aid him with other aspects of his work. For example, the personnel manager may need testing rooms and a large waiting area. If he interviews many applicants each day, it might be important to place his area close to the reception room.

Sales Rooms. If there is need for selling rooms, or display rooms, you will have to know exactly how these rooms are to be used. What is displayed or sold, how much space is required for its storage, and what equipment is needed for its display and storage? Do buyers sit at tables or in auditorium fashion? What other facilities are needed in the room to help the selling or display effort?

Conference Rooms. The questions asked about the conference room in the executive area apply here. In addition, you will want to know who uses the conference room (or rooms) and the type and frequency of meetings in order to determine where it should be located. It will be up to you to help decide whether a department should have its own conference room or whether such a facility can be shared.

Projection Room. Is there need for a projection room in conjunction with a conference room, auditorium, classroom, etc.? If so, what kind of equipment is used? How much storage space must be provided for film, slides, filmstrips, tapes, or other material? The fact that projection equipment is used does not always mean that a special room is required. If such use is infrequent, it would be best not to devote expensive space to it. Equipment can be stored and brought out when needed or disguised and hidden in dozens of ingenious ways.

Library. Where a library is needed you will have to know the lineal footage of shelving required to house the material and the size of the material to be shelved or stored in other ways. You should know if the library is used as a reading and research room or if the material is sent to personnel on request. In order to determine its physical location, you should know by which departments or people it is used most. Are there people in attendance in the library? If so, what kind of equipment do they need? If people come in to work in the library, what kind of equipment do they need and how many people will be using the library at the same time?

Data-processing Room. Much of the information about data-processing requirements will be supplied during interviews with the department head. At this point it is important to know if such a facility is needed, what equipment it must house, whether private or semiprivate offices are required in the area, and what the storage needs are for the room. You will need to know the electrical and air-conditioning requirements for the area. These can be obtained once the manufacturer and model number of each piece of equipment is known, because the manufacturer's catalog will give the electrical needs, the heat load, and the space needed for the machine, as well as the space needed for working and servicing.

File Room and File Equipment. You may have to help make decisions concerning the manner in which the client will handle his filing problems. Will files be kept in individual departments, with individual secretaries, or in a central file room? If there are to be central files, how centrally located must this room be? Will it be attended by file personnel and if so, how many, and what equipment will be needed?

Are files to be legal- or letter-size or a combination of both? How many individual drawers of standard-size files are required? Is the material to be kept in drawers, on shelves, or in some covered system of shelf filing? Has any plan been made to destroy old files on a regular schedule that would affect future file needs? Is there a plan for microfilming, or dead storage of old files? Are worktables needed in the file area? Are there any security problems in connection with files? Are there any security problems anywhere else on the premises?

Telephone and Communication Rooms. The size and type of space required for telephone, intercom, teletype, etc., will depend upon the system or systems that will best serve the client's needs. The variations are too numerous to treat with here, but the planner and designer will, through exposure, become familiar with all of them and will soon be in a position to help the client make decisions in consultation with the telephone company business representative or with specialists in communications systems. Once the requirements are known for the number of trunk lines, the number of extensions, the number of board positions, and the general types of systems to be used (dial 9, switchboard, call director, etc.), the telephone company will help determine the number of feet needed for this facility. The required size should serve your purposes in the first tabulation of client space needs, although more detailed information will be required when you get into the preparation of working drawings.

If there is to be a separate intercom system will its equipment require any space? What equipment for both machines and personnel is required to meet the teletype needs of the client?

Secretarial Pools. Many organizations, instead of assigning secretaries or shared secretaries to some categories of executive personnel, prefer a secretarial pool to handle dictating chores. This can be organized so that the secretary may take dictation at the executive desk or through one of many systems using dictating equipment. If it is agreed that the pool system is a good one, it is then necessary to find out how many pools are required, how many secretaries there are in each, how they are supervised, what would be their most logical physical location, and what kind, number, and type of equipment is required.

Storage Room, Mail and Shipping Room, Reproduction Room—Dark Room. (Although each of these headings is discussed separately, they have been grouped together because in many companies they are best located in the same area, with or without physical separation.) To determine the footage requirements for a storage area, you must know what is to be stored, its size and quantity, and the best method of handling the incoming material in order to get it unpacked, shelved, or otherwise stored in the most expeditious way. You will also want to know, or help determine, how the stored supplies are distributed to the users. It is particularly necessary to know at the outset whether any space-consuming methods, such as dumbwaiters or pneumatic tubes, are being or can be used. If there is a need to store large quantities of material, it would be well to find out how frequently this material is used. Such information will help to determine the type of shelving that should be used and the aisle space that would serve it best, as well as the location of the room itself.

In the mail area you must determine the space requirements for equipment: worktables, mail slots, scales, Pitney-Bowes machines, addressographs, etc. This area will handle both incoming and outgoing mail and other material to be shipped. What kind of personnel is in attendance and what equipment do they need? How is incoming material received and distributed? How is outgoing material collected and shipped?

Printing (multilith, multigraph, etc.) and copying (photostat, blueprint, other dry or wet processes) are often heavy enough activities to warrant central facilities in many organizations. Other companies, with relatively light copying needs, may have one or more copying machines placed within the area or department that has the greatest need for such a facility. If it is a central operation, you will have to know the type, quantity, size, working space, and storage needs (paper, ink, stencils) for each piece of equipment, as well as its heat and electrical load. You should know what supporting equipment, such as worktables, collating machine, and personnel facilities, may be needed.

There may well be a need for a darkroom as part of the copying area or photo studio, if such is required. Here, too, you will have to know the kind of equipment used, as well as its requirements for electricity, gas, and water.

Eating Facilities—Lounge. Is there to be an area where employees can bring their lunch, or a cafeteria where food can be purchased, or a food-vending machine area? Will there be a lounge as part of such areas? You must know the kind of facility and the number of people that will use it, in order to help determine the kind and quantity of equipment that will be required and the footage for housing it. In order to cut down on the size of such facilities in large companies, you may have to help schedule the number and time of servings at each meal period.

Rest Rooms—Sick Bay. Local **labor laws** often dictate the size requirement for rest rooms, but some companies prefer to provide larger facilities. Some supply miniature-hospitals, with nurses in attendance, doctors on call, examination rooms, and rest rooms as well. You must know the type and quantity of equipment needed to fulfill the client's desires. Plumbing and electrical needs will also have to be determined.

Private Toilets, Showers. These facilities have already been mentioned in the discussion of the executive area. There may, however, be a need for such rooms elsewhere in the office space.

Other Special-purpose Rooms. Various kinds of business operations will require special kinds of rooms. The need for them will most likely be revealed during your four-part check on client requirements. In any case, the basic questions must be asked about each room: What is it for, how is it used, how many people work in it, how many people does it have to accommodate, and what kind of equipment is used in it? A complete list of such rooms is almost impossible to compile, but the facilities used most frequently include photo studios, art studios, small theaters, sales classrooms, examination rooms, and interview rooms.

After Hours

If the client's business requires work after the normal workday, you must attempt to plan the space so that the work can be done within a confined area. Since most rental buildings shut off their air-handling equipment after 6:00 or 6:30 at night, your ability to confine the work area will have a direct bearing on the amount of auxiliary air-conditioning equipment necessary to keep the air comfortable. The location of any required facilities for after-hours workers, such as lounges and dining rooms, will also be dependent upon the location of the overtime working area.

Closets

The storage of visitor and personnel clothing presents another important space problem. Personnel clothing can be kept in central coatrooms, locker rooms, department closets, area closets, individual office closets, or back-of-door hooks. The answer will depend upon the number of employees and the size, shape, and number of floors. Visitors' clothing can be kept in a reception-room closet, a conference-room closet, or in the closet of the executive being visited.

Plumbing—Electricity

Are there any space problems concerning the following: sinks, water coolers, time clocks, or other special lighting or electrical equipment?

General

After the interview with the client you may feel that certain basic principles of layout could be used effectively to meet company requirements. Not all clients will be prepared to accept these ideas, even though they may save space or provide other advantages. The ideas listed below should therefore be discussed with the client before an attempt is made to use any of them:

1. Open areas. Each department can be housed behind its own partitions, or many departments can share one large, open area.

2. Window areas. Personnel situated in open areas can be placed next to windows, and private offices can be assigned interior space away from windows.

3. Department supervision. Supervisors and department administrators can be given private offices within, and overlooking, their departments, or they can, instead, share the open area with the department personnel. Status recognition can be given by assigning to the supervisor a greater number of square feet in the open area.

One other thing that should be talked about is the client need for flexibility of layout in order to provide for unpredictable organizational changes. Some companies have no need for this flexibility at all, but others are in a constant state of flux. Flexibility can be provided in several ways, including movable partitions, bank-screened offices, and desk placement in open areas. Your concern with flexibility at this point in your project study relates only to the location of flexible elements and its impact on space needs.

CHECKLIST B   DEPARTMENTAL QUESTIONNAIRE

Many of the questions asked herein will have been covered, in general, in the review with management of Checklist A—Operational Requirements. Going over these again, in more detail, with the person responsible for each department's operation can only add to your overall knowledge of the client's problem.

What is the name of your department?

What does your department do?

What contact do you have with the outside public? (Is there a need to locate this department close to the reception room or to the street floor, or should it have its own public entrance?)

What is the relationship of your department to others; i.e., which departments are in frequent or regular communication with yours, and what is the nature of that communication? (Paper communication will pose one problem, and personnel traffic poses another. Personnel traffic indicates need for physical proximity, but paper communication can be handled in many different mechanical ways.)

How many employees do you now have?

What are the functions of your personnel in each job category?

Do you anticipate an increase of personnel in your department? Why? If possible, can this anticipated growth be classified in job categories?

Do you anticipate an increase of equipment in your department? What equipment has already been purchased but not yet delivered, and what is its expected delivery date? Also what equipment is contemplated to be purchased, and what is the contemplated delivery date?

What records do you store?

Does the volume of stored material increase each year? If so, what is the approximate yearly increase, i.e., half a file drawer, two file drawers, 6 lineal feet of shelving, etc.?

Is there a policy of record retirement into dead storage?

Is there a policy for destroying records? (The last questions are calculated to induce a company with no record policy to initiate one. Records can quickly choke the efficiency of a company, and the problem should be faced by building in an automatic method of control.)

From the personnel list, indication should be made of the kind of space each person in your department is to occupy:

    Private office
    Semiprivate office (two to four people in an enclosed area)
    Desk in open area

Do you have need for a department conference room?

If so, how many people should it accommodate at a conference table? How often would this room be used each day? Each week?

Do you have any other special space needs for waiting, storage, or other purposes?

CHECKLIST C   INVENTORY

The inventory list will, in all probability, become an inventory form when used by the planner and designer. The design of the form is left to the individual designer. Listed here are those items that should be included on this form.

    Name of client
    Job number
    Date of inventory taking
    Department (or other unit)

Personnel

    (Each person whose equipment is being inventoried should be listed by name and title, and each person should be given the identification number previously discussed. This will help to check on the number of people in each department, and it will also provide an easy way to list those people who should be located near each other.)

Existing

Type of space
(Is the space now being used a private office, semiprivate office, open area, etc.?)

Quantity and item
(Desk, table, key punch, chair, files, etc.)

Size of items—width, depth, height
(Measurements need not be taken of anything not occupying floor space, such as adding machines on tables or typewriters on desks.)

Condition—(New, good, or poor)

Telephone—
(Is instrument needed at desk and elsewhere in room?)

Electrical facilities
(Equipment for which it is needed. Power required if it is in excess of normal outlet output, and if it requires separate circuiting.)

Proposed

(This general category will be used for equipment to be purchased for expansion purposes, as well as equipment to be purchased, or proposed to be purchased, as replacement for old or inefficient equipment.)

Type of space
(This may be a repeat of the information shown under **Existing** type of space or it may indicate a change.)

Locate near
(This should be used for indicating the desired working relationship of personnel within departments or units as well as relationships between departments. Use the identification numbers to indicate these relationships.)

Quantity and item
(These two columns should be left blank if the equipment is the same as that listed under **Existing**.)

(Frequently the planner and designer will use the inventory form as a work sheet for calculating footage requirements. If the form is so used, it would be wise to have a column under **Existing** for footage now being used and one under **Proposed** for footage required. By assigning footage to each person and to each piece of equipment, it will be easy to arrive at total department footage now being used and the total of net footage required in new offices.)

Before leaving this inventory list it would be well to discuss some possible shortcuts that can be taken in using it. There are many standard items that will be inventoried. In fact, most items are of standard sizes and materials. Legends can be set up covering these standards so that filling in the form will be a little easier. Four-drawer letter files, for example, can be indicated as "4 dr. let." A wood, secretarial typing desk with right-pedestal typing can be shown as W-ST-R. The legend can cover type of space, desks, chairs, files, tables, condition of furniture, and in fact anything the planner and designer wishes it to cover. The legend should be used only for constantly repeated items of equipment. Too big a legend can become almost unworkable.

Some planners and designers have designed their forms with columns for the types and sizes of equipment repeated most often. Then the items need only be checked off, rather than otherwise noted on the inventory form. This method leads to errors, however, when the check mark inadvertently lands in the wrong column.

CHECKLIST D   DESIGN AND CONSTRUCTION REQUIREMENTS

This checklist is handled like the others in this book, with explanations given wherever the listed item requires it. The list, which should be used after all the aesthetic aims of the client have been discussed, is divided into two sections. The first covers items normally considered as basic construction items, and the second part is concerned with items for design and purchase. Overlapping is unavoidable, because some items can fall under either category, depending upon the specific demands of a particular job. For example, a clothes closet can be a routine construction installation on one job or a highly designed, costly cabinetwork installation on another.

Very often the items on this list will be discussed with the client after the space study has been completed. When that happens, the study can be checked off, room by room, to make certain that every area has been reviewed.

In those cases where the client is planning to move into space he will be renting, many of the construction items on the checklist will be supplied at no cost to him. This will have been so indicated in the work-letter portion of his lease. These items will be standard to the entire building and not subject to client or designer choice, unless there is a wish to substitute for **building standard** and pay for the dif-

*Checklist D
Design
and
Construction
Requirements*

ference in cost. The entire subject of lease and work letter will be covered in Chapter III.

The items on this list should be discussed with the client for any specific requirements he may have concerning them. When anything in either of the lists is to be included in the budget as a cost to the client, determination will have to be made of the quantity of each item in terms of number of units, square feet, linear feet, weight, or any other pricing unit.

CONSTRUCTION

1. **Partitions**
   Block-and-plaster, steel, steel-and-glass, Dri-wall, etc. Design decisions must be made concerning the types of partitions that are to be used in addition to or in place of building-standard walls. The necessity for flexibility in layout and movability of partitions must be thoroughly explored.

2. **Doors, Bucks, and Hardware**
   Herculite, hollow metal, wood, etc.
   7 foot height or ceiling height.
   Sliding doors for clothes and storage closets.
   Wood or metal bucks.
   Latch sets, locks, stops, surface-mounted checks, concealed checks.

3. **Ceilings**
   Acoustical tile, plaster, acoustic plaster, etc.
   Type of suspension system.

4. **Flooring**
   Asphalt tile, vinyl, vinyl asbestos, linoleum, cork, etc.
   Base of tile, rubber, etc.
   Coved or straight base.

5. **Lighting**
   Fixtures for general lighting (fluorescent and incandescent), exit lights.

6. **Electrical Facilities**
   Duplex outlets, switches, dimmers, outlets for special equipment, IBM equipment, clocks, under-floor ducts, outlets for audio, TV, intercom.

7. **Telephone Requirements**
   Switchboard, centrex, dial 9, etc.
   Number of stations, conduits, etc.
   The telephone company business representative should be consulted concerning the type of system that should be used. He should also be notified (by the client) of the planned moving date, so that equipment,

not normally delivered rapidly, can be ordered as early as possible. The cost of installation must also come from the telephone company.

Intercom through telephone system or separate system, including voice or visual paging system.

8. **Plumbing**

   Water coolers, sinks, kitchens, pantries, private toilets, showers, darkrooms, etc.

9. **Heating, Ventilating, and Air Conditioning**

   Smoke exhaust for kitchens, heat-producing equipment, conference rooms, etc.

   Reheat units for conference rooms and auditoriums.

   Independent systems for areas in use after working hours.

10. **Painting**
11. **Carpentry**

    Hat shelves and clothes rods for closets.

12. **Material Handling**

    Pneumatic-tube system, dumbwaiter, belt, etc.

Design-purchase Items. In discussing this section of the checklist it is always easier to talk about each room or area in the space being designed, making sure that each applicable item on the list has been covered. For example, instead of asking which rooms are to be carpeted, it is better to go through the operational requirements taken earlier and ask, during a discussion of the president's office, whether it is to be carpeted. Then, during a discussion of the conference room, determine the flooring to be used there, etc.

To show how a typical room-by-room discussion encompasses many of the items on the checklist, these are examples of the questions that should be asked.

1. Explain your need for (or lack of need for) a desk or other work area or surface.

2. How many seats must be provided in this office for visitors?

3. Do you want a comfortable lounge area in the office?

4. Do you require conference space? At table?

5. What storage facilities do you need for papers, books, or other items?

6. Do you need file space?

7. Do you require pin-up space or chalkboard or projection equipment?

Checklist D Design and Construction Requirements

8. Is there need for television or hi-fi or bar facilities?
9. Do you have any special lighting needs?
10. Should desks or storage areas be provided with locks?
11. Do you have any artwork or anything else of a special nature that must be provided for in the room?
12. Do you have any particular desire for a specific wall material?
13. Do you have any particular desire for a specific flooring?
14. Should draperies be used at the windows?

The same questions can be asked about each room and area in the total space. In Chapter III, the desirability of using some of these elements, such as displays in a reception room, will be discussed. Your immediate interest is in knowing if the client has any preconceived ideas about these items.

Walls
Paneling, Flexwood, grass cloth, vinyl, wood and glass

Flooring
Carpet, wood, ceramic tile, marble, terrazzo
Reducing strips between carpet and noncarpet area

Electrical
Incandescent, fluorescent, cove lights, chandeliers, wall fixtures, directional lights

Window Treatments
Blinds, shades, curtains, draperies

Clothing Storage
Closets, racks, rooms

Furniture
Desks, chairs, tables, sofas, settees, benches

In discussing furniture and equipment, decisions should be reached concerning standardization of both. Standardization can blanket an entire company or it can include only certain levels of work categories. Any purchasing program that is planned to spread out over a number of years will have to take into account as much furniture and equipment standardization as possible.

Equipment
Files, wastebaskets, ashtrays, plants, mirrors, pictures, desk sets, clocks, other accessories

Conference-room Facilities
Projection room, telephone room, display boards, chalkboards, corkboard, movie screen

Private Toilet, Rest-room Equipment
Medicine chest, cot, sanitary equipment, toilet-paper holder, towel bar

Recreational Facilities
Sauna room, lounges, dining areas, bars, cellarettes, refrigerators, glasses, dishes, cabinets

Storage and Mail-room Equipment
Worktables, shelving

Display, Showroom Equipment
Furniture, display cabinets, display racks

Special Facilities
Locks on cabinets, desks, tables
Drawers in desks, tables, cabinets
Drawer divisions for files, pencil trays, etc.
Switchboard enclosure
Soundproof enclosures for teletypes and other noisy equipment
Pull-out slides for desks, tables, or work areas

Signs

Moving
(Included to make certain it is made part of the budget)

CHAPTER II ANALYZING

To analyze the possible approaches to the client's housing problem, to compare the financial aspects of each approach, and to investigate space utilization is the second major step in an office-planning project. The number of square feet required for the client's operation is the basic information necessary for this analysis.

Space standards will be established and square feet tabulated after you have completed searching and questioning and examining the client's business. This probing will broaden your exposure to other specialists who will have contributions to make to your analysis of the problem: the real estate consultant, the landlord, the architect, the mechanical and structural engineers, the contractors, and the municipal authorities. You will study the collected data, weigh the advantages and disadvantages of renting space, building it, or remodeling it, and search for the answers that will allow the space you plan to stand the test of use. ■

SECTION I ANALYZING THE AMOUNT OF SPACE REQUIRED

The information you compiled when you reviewed the questions listed in Chapter I's checklists will be used in preparing a **tabulation of the square feet** required to house the client's company. The tabulation is the foundation for the project itself, and will be part of your **report** to the client. This report is so vital that the information, the assumptions, the interpretations, and the tabulations upon which its conclusions are based must be carefully scrutinized by management and discussed with them before you proceed with the next phase of effort.

The nature and size of the report analyzing the client's problem will depend entirely upon the simplicity or complexity of the project. Its physical form will be a matter of individual designer taste and creativity. A simple form for reporting an organization's requirements is shown on page 65 of Chapter III. A more complex report could contain all or part of the information described in Section III of this chapter.

If you know that many of the conclusions in the report are based on your own assumptions (or the assumptions of those questioned) and that management may make many changes, it would be well to make the first report a preliminary one. Whether the report be preliminary or final, it must be planned so that the information that led to your conclusions can be easily checked and validated by management.

To accomplish this the report must include:

1. A full description of the client operation

2. The **space standards** recommended to meet the operational requirements

3. The tabulation of the total number of square feet required to house the operation

The description of the operation will be a compendium of all that you have learned from interviews and tours through the client's space. It would be well to set up the report in the same way you organized the interviews and the inventory, department by department. Care must be taken to keep all departmental nomenclature and any identifying numerical references to individuals or divisional units the same throughout the report. Variations can cause unfortunate confusion.

Departmental descriptions should contain the name of the person or persons originally interviewed and should record the factual information gathered concerning the existing operation, as well as any information given about expected, projected, or desired departmental expansion or contraction. The report must also record the interrelationships of departments and intrarelationships of people within departments as you understand them. It is within these areas of projections and relationships particularly that you must look to management for agreement or correction.

The second part of the report consists of the drawings and descriptive prose necessary to illustrate the space standards suggested for all work and service areas. A representative group of such standards is illustrated on pages 46 and 48. The drawings show space allotments for furniture and equipment found in most offices. Use of the word "standard" does not mean that one company's standard will be the same as the next. It might be well to take a look at the way in which room requirements are interpreted into what would be standards.

One law firm, with a number of senior partners, wanted each to have a comfortable office with a desk, sofa, lounge chair, a few pull-up chairs, and as much work surface as possible. Drawing 1, showing these requirements, would be included in the report to this client as a standard A office. Associate partners and juniors were assigned standards of B offices (150 square feet) and C offices (100 square feet).

Another law firm, with a number of senior partners, wanted each to have what the partners in the first firm were to get, plus space for a conference table seating six people. Each partner, because of the nature of the firm's practice, had need for this facility. So the standard A office for the firm had to contain 330 square feet (Drawing 2), with the B and C offices sized for their respective needs.

In addition to establishing sizes for all private offices and for the special-purpose rooms such as reception rooms and storage rooms, space must be allotted to standard office operations (work stations) and equipment (files, storage cabinets). A representative few of those that are used most often are shown on Drawing 3. These and all of the other work stations and space-taking furniture and equipment specific to each project should be illustrated in the report in order to clearly show the client exactly how and why you arrived at your footage allotments.

The third part of the report is the actual tabulation of square feet needed to properly house the client company. Sometimes the report will include the complete inventory of furniture and equipment. If so, the in-

Drawing 1

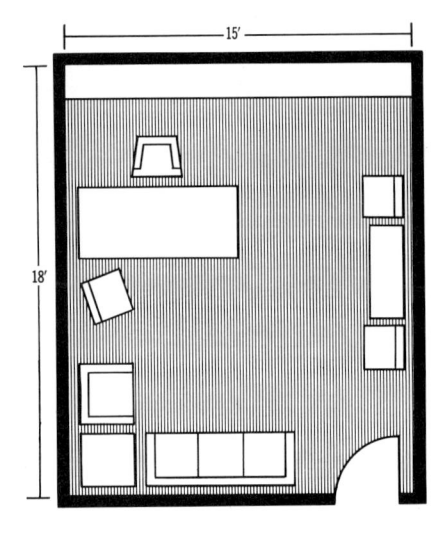

SPACE STANDARDS
Private Office — 270 square feet

This office, that of a senior partner in a law firm, is planned to meet his working and seating requirements. The oversized desk (7 by 3 feet) and the room-width work surface in back of him accommodate his need for "spread" space. Cabinets underneath the rear work surface and a bookcase on the long wall to his left provide space for his books and paper storage. Three pull-up chairs, a sofa, and a lounge chair meet the seating requirements of the office.

Drawing 2

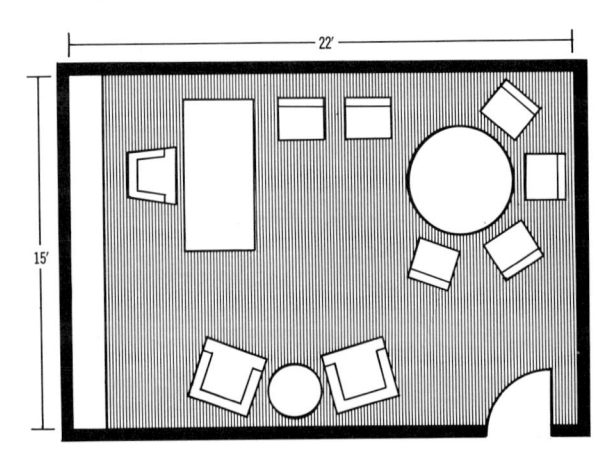

SPACE STANDARDS
Private Office — 330 square feet

This office is also planned to house a senior partner in a law firm but one with different requirements from those illustrated on Drawing 1. Instead of a sofa and lounge chair, the comfortable seating has been reduced to two lounge chairs, so that space could be provided to accommodate a required conference table.

A 6-foot desk has been substituted for the 7-foot desk, and book storage space has been provided in the cabinet along the rear wall.

ventory can be used as your work sheet, with the footage required for each work station tabulated in the "proposed" section of the form. The assigned footages will be taken from the standards already set. If it is not necessary to include the inventory sheets in the report, a simplified tabulation form can be used as the footage work sheet. Such a **tabulation form** is described in **Checklist E** at the end of this chapter.

Whether the footages are on the inventory sheets or on the tabulation form, the report must contain a clear, concise summary of the total footage requirements. One way to do this is to use a columnar form, with the first column used to list the names of all departments and service areas. The **usable footage** of the existing space will be listed in the second column. The third column will show the net usable footage required for the expanded department, and the fourth column will show the total usable footage required to house each department, including a 15 percent **factor** added to take care of intradepartmental traffic. This 15 percent factor represents the percentage of square feet allotted within a department for the aisles and equipment work space needed by the department's personnel for their own and visitor circulation. It is an average percentage arrived at from an analysis of the circulation figures used on many planning projects. At the bottom of the page all departmental requirements, plus the 15 percent factor, will be totaled, and another factor of 10 percent will then be added for interdepartmental corridors. This percentage is also an average, arrived at after the study of hundreds of completed jobs, and represents the required circulation area for personnel traffic between departments, **building core,** and service areas. The final total of departmental requirements, plus 15 percent, plus 10 percent will give us the usable footage required for layout. The manner in which these figures are to be used in determining renting or building requirements will be discussed in the next section of this chapter.

SECTION II   ANALYZING THE DIRECTION: RENT, BUILD, OR REMODEL

Once the report and the tabulation of required footage have been accepted by management, the information can be used in your analysis of

Drawings 3a–d

SPACE STANDARDS
Work Stations, Furniture, and Equipment

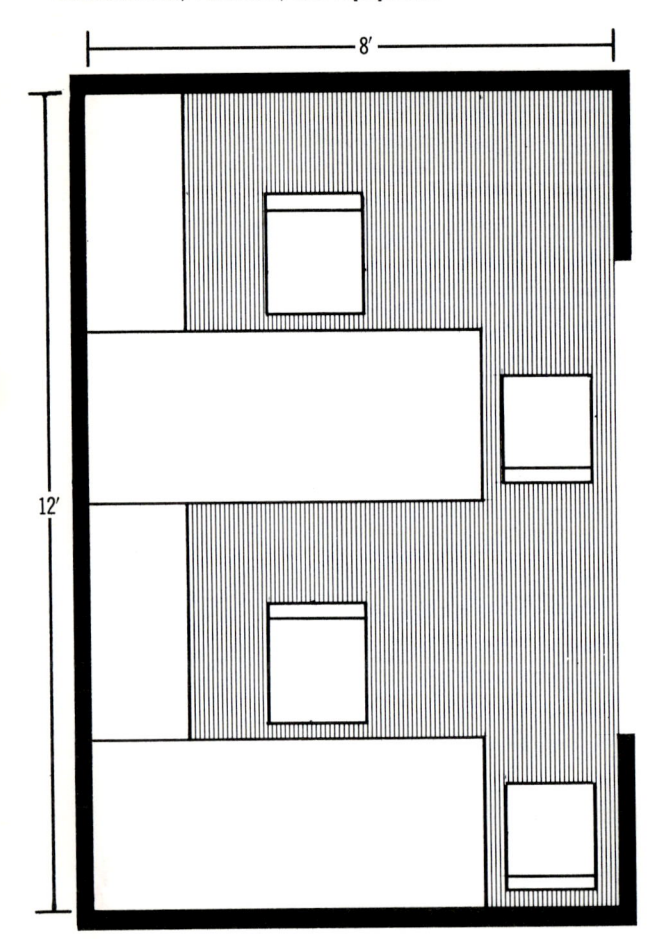

a. Enclosed Work Station: 2 Men, 96 sq ft.

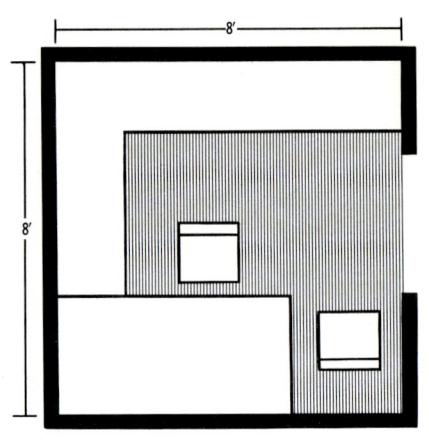

b. Enclosed Work Station: 1 Man, 64 sq ft.

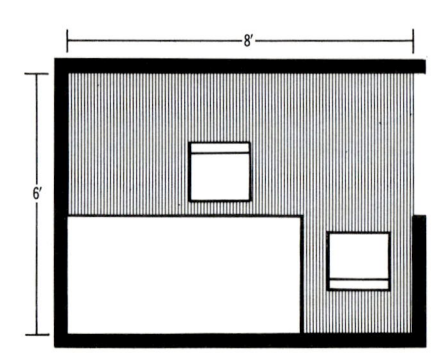

c. Enclosed Work Station: 1 Man, 48 sq ft.

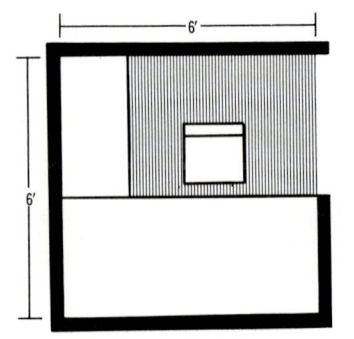

d. Enclosed Work Station: 1 Man, 36 sq ft.

the direction toward which the client may go: whether to rent, build, or remodel.

Not all situations will require an analysis of direction. There will be times when the decision will be dictated by circumstances. A steel company in Hamilton, Ontario, had office facilities in many small buildings on their widespread plant property. As they grew, it became less and less efficient for them to have executive, engineering, sales, and purchasing offices so widely separated. None of the buildings then occupied by offices was large enough to house the entire office complex, nor were there any other structures on the property capable of being renovated for this purpose. There were no office buildings in town that could house the company's requirements. Obviously they would have to build, and since their own property was large enough to accommodate them, they would build on it. Because a major highway bisected their property, it was decided to build the new office building near the highway. This would provide easy access and would take advantage of the public relations and institutional advertising value to be gained from having a new building visible to the passing traffic.

When there is no such clear-cut situation, the space planner must make a complete analysis of all the possibilities open to his client and must evaluate the advantages and disadvantages of renting, building, and remodeling.

An analysis of renting must start with the conversion of required usable footage into the number of feet for which the client would have to pay rent. In some cities usable footage in office buildings is the same as **rentable**. In others, there is a percentage factor difference between usable and rentable. The factor may vary from city to city, as well as from building to building.

The geographical variations in approach to basic **floor measurements** usually come from the particular rules and regulations of the local real estate board or from the rules and regulations of the Building Owners and Managers Association (BOMA), which have been adopted in many localities. The variation in measurements from one building to another in one geographical locality stems from the physical variations of each building, which can include the number and size of elevators, toilets, and air-conditioning equipment rooms.

Drawings 3e–h

SPACE STANDARDS
Work Stations, Furniture, and Equipment (cont.)

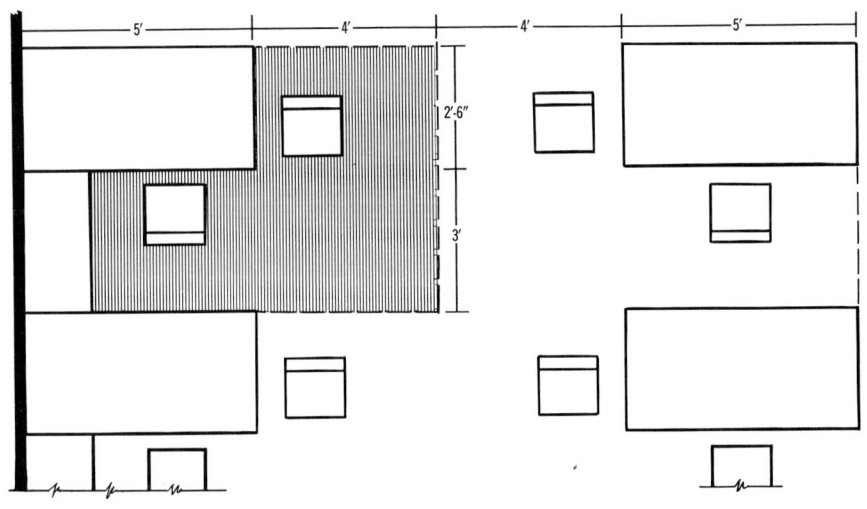

e. *Open Area Work Stations: Desks with visitor chairs, with and without "L" units.*

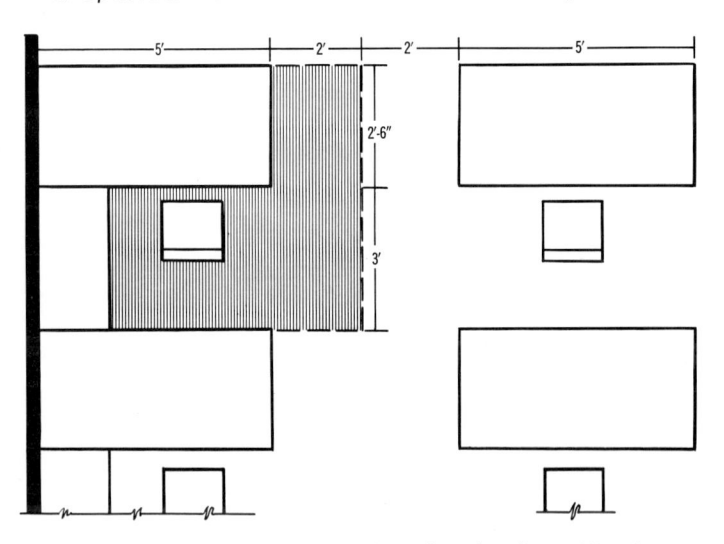

f. *Open Area Work Stations: Desks with and without "L" units.*

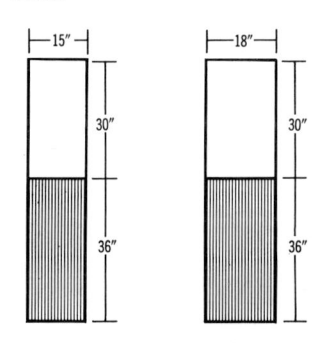

g. *File Cabinets. (Left) Letter Size with work space; (Right) Legal Size with work space.*

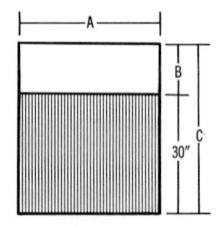

h. *Shelf Unit, Bookcase or Side File, with work space.*

Analyzing the Direction: Rent, Build, or Remodel

Before calculating any measurements you must be sure that you know whose rules and regulations are to be followed. In case of doubt, this can be checked with the local real estate board. In New York City, the real estate board says that all measurements are to be taken from the inside glass line of windows and, where there are no windows, from the inside line of the outside building wall or demising wall. BOMA, on the other hand, ignores glass lines entirely, and all its measurements are taken from the inside line of peripheral walls.

No matter whose rules and regulations are used, measurements should always be taken from dimensioned architectural drawings or actual field dimensions. They should not be made from **rental plans,** which are rarely accurate and usually oversimplified to make them more comprehensible to potential tenants.

Using a scale rule on undimensioned drawings increases the inaccuracies. The chance for error is so great in reading dimensions from a scale ruler that it is almost impossible for any two people to ever come up with the same answer.

Drawing 4 illustrates the New York City Real Estate Board rules for measuring office-building floors. It is quite apparent from an examination of this drawing that the usable footage on this floor is not the same as the rentable. In order to convert the usable feet to rentable, it is necessary to obtain the rental schedule from the building owner. This particular floor, measured by Real Estate Board standards, contains 5,250 square feet of rentable space. For the sake of illustrating the way in which usable is converted to rentable for partial floor users, assume that the client needs 2,500 square feet of usable space. The usable square feet on the floor (the white space on Drawing 4) totals 4,040 square feet. The difference between 4,040 square feet (usable) and 5,250 square feet (rentable) is calculated as a factor of 1.3 (usable times factor equals rentable). Now take the 2,500 square feet that the client needs, multiply it by 1.3, and you learn that to get his 2,500 usable square feet, he must actually rent 3,250 square feet.

If the client were to use the entire floor, he would get more usable feet than the 4,040 measure for the divided floor, because added to that footage would be the corridor area in front of the elevators. This becomes his to use as the single occupant of the floor.

Drawing 4

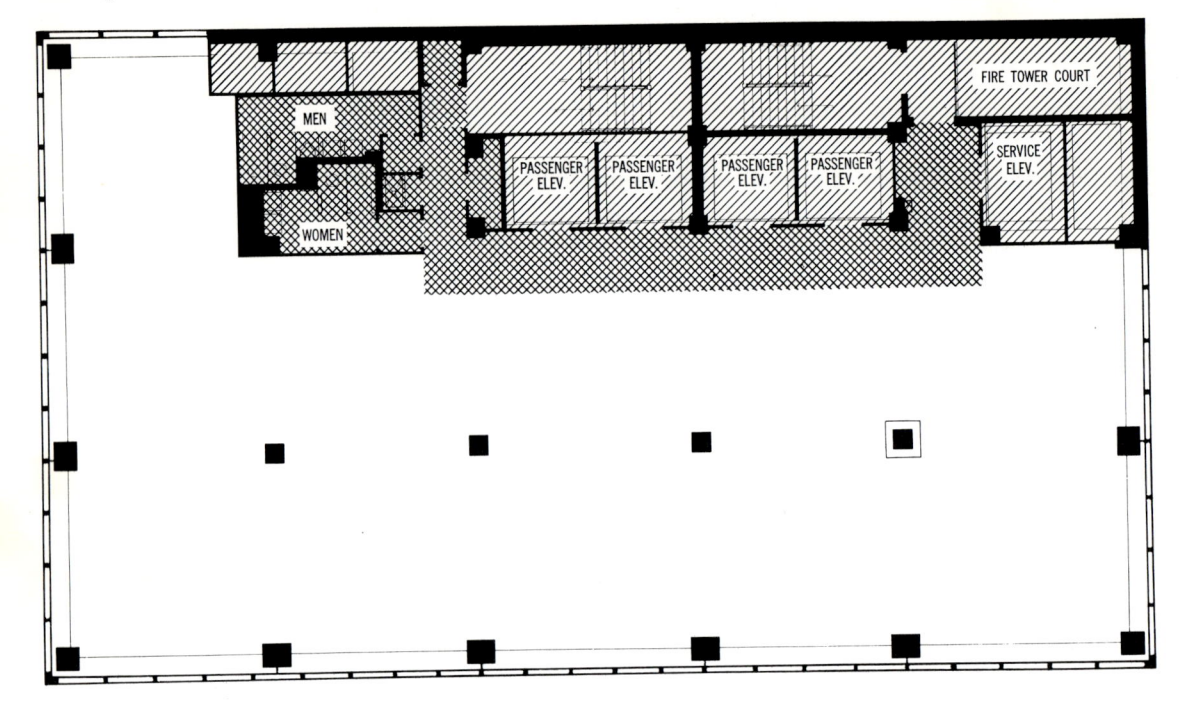

FLOOR MEASUREMENT FOR SINGLE AND DIVIDED TENANCY
Plan Showing Standard Method of Floor Measurement
for Office Buildings

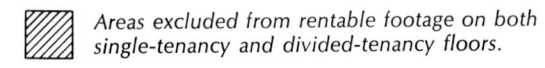

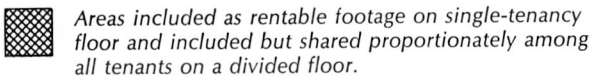

▨ *Areas excluded from rentable footage on both single-tenancy and divided-tenancy floors.*

▩ *Areas included as rentable footage on single-tenancy floor and included but shared proportionately among all tenants on a divided floor.*

All other areas are rentable including columns. The areas excluded from rentable footage in Drawing 4 are the public stairs, fire towers, public elevator shafts, flues, vents, stacks, pipe shafts, and vertical ducts. The areas included as rentable footage on single-tenancy floors are toilets, janitors' closets, slop sinks, and electrical and telephone closets. For divided floors the same areas listed above are included as rentable but shared proportionately by all tenants on the floor. The shared areas on a divided floor also include public corridors and elevator corridors.

Also included as rentable, according to the New York City Real Estate Board, should be the tenant's proportionate share of air-conditioning rooms and fan rooms that serve his space, even though the rooms are located on floors other than his.

Analyzing the Direction: Rent, Build, or Remodel

On multiple-occupancy floors the width of the corridor in front of the elevator is fixed by local **building codes** only insofar as its minimum width is concerned. For the sake of appearance, most building elevator corridors are wider than called for by minimum code requirements, with the width usually fixed by the building owner.

Having converted required usable footage into rentable footage, there is one more figure to compute before proceeding with your analysis of the possible housing alternatives open to the client company. That figure is the conversion of usable footage into the total number of square feet that would be required to build a new building.

To arrive at a preliminary gross building footage (and it is, of course, preliminary subject to the later development of actual plans) that includes the building core (toilets, stairwells, shafts, etc.) and all **building service areas,** you should add a factor of 25 percent to the required usable total.

With the relative sizes of area to be built and area to be rented established, the cost of each must now be examined. The initial examination is aimed at finding out, before getting too deeply involved in an unnecessary amount of work, whether building is financially feasible. You have the footage required for the building; you must now know how much the land will cost and how much it will cost to build on that land. A study of the departmental footage will help to establish the approximate desired size and height of the building (as described in Section III of this chapter) and, in turn, help to determine land requirements.

Time now to use the specialized help of the **realtor.** When advised of client's land needs, which include desirable location as well as size, he should be able to tell the client and you what is available, where, and for how much. He should be able to supply the figure on the amount of cash required and the amount of money needed annually for interest and amortization of the mortgage. The next important information will come from the **general contractor.** Basing his calculations on a broad description of the hypothetical building, he should be able to estimate the dollars per square foot needed to construct the building.

If the client intends to use a local company to manage the building, that company will supply the figures for such management. If the client wants to do his own maintenance and management, Building Owners and Managers Association (BOMA) will make available these cost figures.

Planning by Design

If costs for land, building, and maintenance indicate an expenditure within the capabilities of the client, it then becomes necessary to go more deeply into a detailed comparison of all the housing methods open to the client company.

An outline of an **evaluation report,** which includes such comparisons, is shown in **Checklist F** at the end of this chapter on page 58. Much of the information in the report is acquired when you take the steps described in Chapter III concerning the preparation of the space study and budget. The other steps are described in the following section.

SECTION III ANALYZING A PROGRAM FOR A NEW BUILDING

If the decision for housing the client indicates the feasibility of building for his own occupancy, recommendations must be made concerning the size, shape, and number of floors that will best meet his organizational needs. The requirement report supplies all the information needed to develop the program for the building. The description of the client's operation gives an understanding of the departmental relationships that must be an integral part of the new building, and the space standards and tabulation of square feet needed for each department allow you to affix the perimeters of the space that will represent departmental areas.

If you are good at your trade, there can be no controversy over your analysis of the client's functional requirements and the blocks of space needed to meet those requirements. Building design must then conform to the needs of the occupant (Mies van der Rohe once said that a building must work like a machine from the inside out) or it will subvert those needs for something other than the avowed purpose for building the building in the first place.

Armed with the informational guidelines, you can begin to work out alternate **building schemes** in both **block** and **tabular form.** Each of the schemes must reveal your understanding of the working relationships of the various departments. The elements of operation that affect the physical location of departments are those concerned with traffic to a department from outside the company, as well as personnel and paper traffic between or within departments. Operational requirements are not always met by placing departments next to each other on a horizontal plane. Sometimes, when department size or floor size indicates, it may be best to accommodate the required relationships on a vertical plane, with one department above another. Drawings 5, 6, and 7 show how this is done on building block layouts.

Several alternate schemes based on the actual requirements of a steel company are described in tabular form and illustrated in block or building cross sections. The site for our building allowed for a maximum floor size of about 25,000 square feet. The tabulation of client's needs indicated a building of 90,000 to 100,000 square feet, which immediately ruled out anything less than four floors for the new building.

The three alternate schemes meet the required departmental relationships: two of them utilize four floors each and one uses five floors. All dimensions have been rounded out to even numbers. The accompanying building elevations give visual illustrations of each scheme, with the arrows showing how required departmental relationships are maintained either horizontally or vertically.

Scheme 1 FOUR-STORY BUILDING

	Sq Ft
Basement	
Parking	10,000
Testing	3,500
File, storage, printing	4,500
Building services	6,500
	24,500
First Floor	
Reception, conference	1,500
Cafeteria	5,000
Metallurgy	3,000
Engineering	10,500
Building services	2,500
	22,500
Second Floor	
Sales	7,000
Purchasing	5,500
Library, conference, auditorium	3,000
Quality control	4,500
Building services	2,500
	22,500

Drawing 5

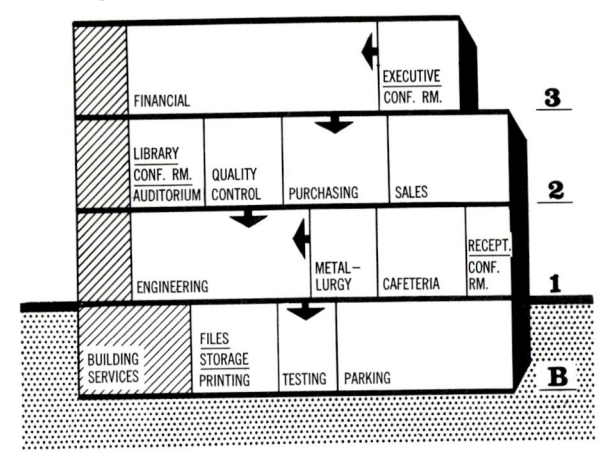

ALTERNATE BUILDING SCHEME 1

Cross section showing departmental relationships in a four-story building. Required relationships, indicated by arrows, are maintained either horizontally or vertically.

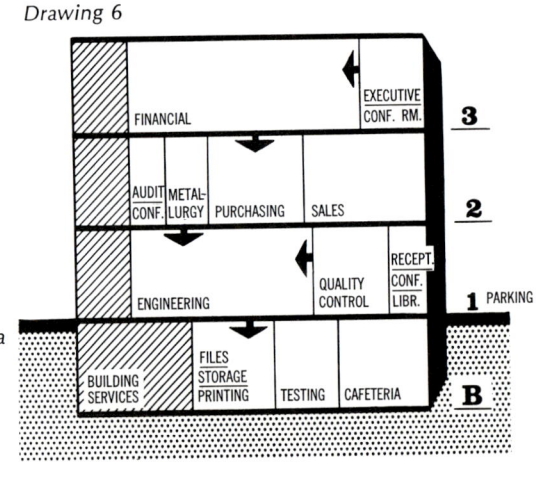

ALTERNATE BUILDING SCHEME 2

Cross section showing departmental relationships in a four-story building.

Drawing 6

Drawing 7

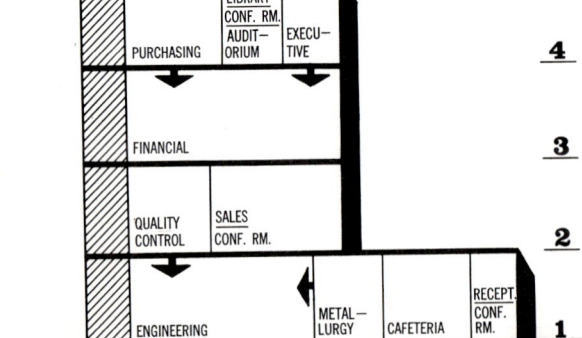

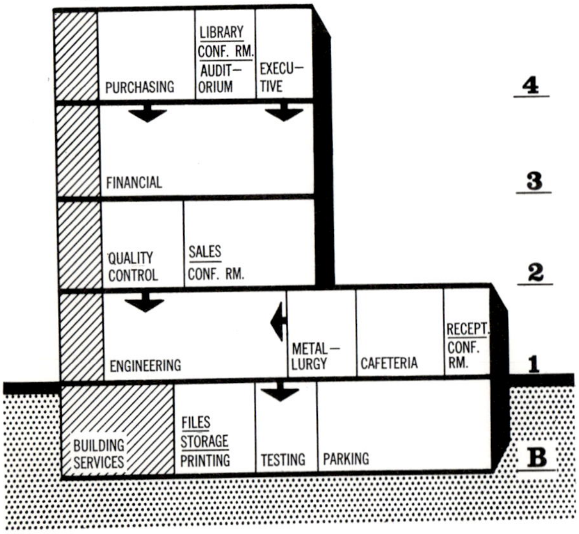

ALTERNATE BUILDING SCHEME 3

Cross section showing departmental relationships in a five-story building.

Third Floor

Executive	2,900
Financial	14,500
Conference room	600
Building services	2,500
	20,500

Scheme 2 FOUR-STORY BUILDING

Basement	**Sq Ft**
Parking Outside	
File, storage, printing	4,500
Cafeteria	5,000
Testing	3,500
Building services	6,500
	19,500

First Floor

Reception, conference	1,500
Engineering	10,500
Quality control	4,500
Library	1,000
Building services	2,500
	20,000

Second Floor

Conference, auditorium	2,000
Metallurgy	3,000
Purchasing	5,500
Sales	7,000
Building services	2,500
	20,000

Third Floor

Executive	2,900
Financial	14,500
Conference room	600
Building services	2,500
	20,500

Scheme 3 FIVE-STORY BUILDING

Basement	**Sq Ft**
Parking	10,000
File, storage, printing	4,500
Testing	3,500
Building services	6,500
	24,500

First Floor

Reception, conference	1,500
Cafeteria	5,000
Metallurgy	3,000
Engineering	10,500
Building services	2,500
	22,500

Analyzing a Program for a New Building

Second Floor
Quality control	4,500
Sales	7,000
Conference	600
Building services	2,500
	14,600

Third Floor
Financial	14,500
Building services	2,500
	17,000

Fourth Floor
Executive	2,900
Purchasing	5,500
Library, conference, auditorium	3,000
Building services	2,500
	13,900

One last word concerning the written documents that have been discussed in this chapter. The reporting vehicle that explains the analysis of the client's problems does not consist of many reports but is instead a cumulative one made up of many parts, with each added as it is required. Each report will contain:

1. Departmental descriptions.
2. Space standards.
3. Tabulation of square feet. This would be shown on the inventory form (Checklist C), on the tabulation form (Checklist E), or as a simple listing of departments with the required footage for each.

If the analysis includes a comparison of renting, remodeling, or building possibilities, the document will also contain:

4. Program for a building.
5. Space studies of all areas being analyzed.
6. Evaluation report (Checklist F).

The space studies (item 5 above) are usually too large to be bound with the report and would instead be supporting documents accompanying the report. Inventory sheets, if they are included, would be either bound with the report or in separate, additional volumes.

In addition, each report should contain:

7. A table of contents.
8. A description of objectives and procedures.
9. A summation of conclusions and recommendations.

*Checklist E 57
Tabulation
Form*

Remember that the conclusions in the report and the recommendations you are making based upon those conclusions will begin a chain of events that will involve the client in a large expenditure of money and you in the myriad of details attendant upon a client move. It would be well to arrange one or two interim meetings with the client during the preparation of the report, so that all assumptions will be carefully checked before you make your final recommendations. Once the questioned details have been agreed upon, it is important that the report be a clear, concise, and definitive document, because not only must it explain your conclusions to the client, but it will be the basic program for all of the work necessary to prepare the new home for client occupancy.

CHECKLIST E   TABULATION FORM

This form should be used if the inventory form (Checklist C) is not made part of the report. It may also be used as a recapitulation of the inventory forms on large jobs when inventory sheets are too numerous for easy handling. A separate sheet (or sheets) should be used for each department or divisional unit. The form should contain:

Name of client
Name of department
Name of department head
Number of square feet presently occupied
Thumbnail description of department function and relationship to other departments or people

The following information should be columnized:

1. Type of space or equipment

This would list private office A, B, etc., semiprivate office, bank-screen office, etc. In outside areas and general-office areas you would list all space-taking equipment such as desks, letter files, legal files, chairs, etc. Also list departmental storage rooms, conference rooms, etc.

2. Assigned square footage per unit

Here you would list the number of square feet for each private office—A, B, etc.—and for all the space and equipment listed in column 1. The number of square feet for each would represent the footage illustrated in the space-standard section of your report.

3. **Number of units required**
   Enter in this column the required number of each item listed in column 1.

4. **Square feet required**
   Column 2 multiplied by column 3.

5. **Remarks**
   Use this column for any required explanatory information.

At the bottom of the page total the footages in column 4, and add 15 percent to that amount to take care of intradepartmental traffic requirements. This represents the departmental total required for layout and should be entered as the final figure on the page.

At times the analysis you are making may have to include provisions for tabulating desired expansion. The future needs would be tabulated for a particular year in the future or in steps (such as five-year intervals) until that future year is reached. In order to use this form for such comparative tabulations, you need simply repeat columns 3 and 4 for each expansion step. Of course, at the bottom of each column 4 you must add the 15 percent factor.

CHECKLIST F   EVALUATION REPORT

The purpose of the report is to compare the advantages and disadvantages of renting, or remodeling, or building a new structure for the client's use.

Space-study plans (the preparation of which are described in Chapter III) of the space to be remodeled and of the space or spaces to be considered for renting should be part of the report, as should the study made of any hypothetical new building.

The comparative studies should all utilize the same basic space requirements that were gathered from the client, and each should include the same expansion provisions. In addition, identical environmental elements should be included in each of the compared situations. It would be well for the report to list them, in order to assure that none had been overlooked. These would include partitions, doors, hardware, acoustical ceilings, and all the other elements listed in

Checklist F 59
Evaluation
Report

Checklist D—Design and Construction Requirements on page 36, plus any others that may apply to a particular company.

The following items could then be compared, supported by the actual space studies:

1. **Efficiency of layout**
    This would compare the problems or lack of problems in effecting a smooth operation within the physical capacities of each space.

2. **Functional relationship of departmental areas**
    This comparison would be supported by the space studies which would help reveal the adequacy or inadequacy of each building in providing proper departmental location.

3. **The square footage required**
    This comparison would be concerned only with the possible variation of usable square feet as measured against rentable square feet in each space being considered for renting or the gross footage on which rent would be paid in a structure being built for client use.

4. **Ability to absorb expansion efficiently**
    This would show the comparative advantages and disadvantages of the physical location of expansion space in its relationship to the departments for which space should be provided.

5. **Ability to provide for future needs**
    In addition to comparing the core and any peripheral rigidity that may later cause difficulty in plan changes, you should be concerned with the specifics of client requirements such as:
    (a) Automation equipment and the electrical capacity to cope with it.
    (b) Material-handling equipment and the ability to accommodate it in a horizontal or vertical plan.
    (c) After-hours air conditioning, which may eventually have to be provided.

6. **Analysis of building facilities**
    This section would compare and analyze the elevators, toilets, parking, public traffic areas, mechanical facilities, and storage availability in each of the locations being considered.

7. **Cost of interior improvements**
    Assuming that furniture, furnishings, cabinetwork, etc., would be the same no matter where the client eventually goes, comparison must be made of costs of basic interior construction elements. The manner in which this would be budgeted is covered in Section II of Chapter III. The costs in a landlord-owned building will vary according to the amount of work

the landlord may be willing to do for the client under the terms of his lease. This, too, is described in Section II of Chapter III. Costs for basic interior work in the building created for single occupancy will be part of the initial cost of construction.

8. Time factor for completion
This would be a comparison of construction time schedules.

9. Operating efficiency during construction
A discussion of the problems involved in working while construction is going on in a remodeling situation must take into consideration the psychological effect on employees of walking into and working in a new building.

The "moment of truth," however, comes with the comparison of costs—the dollars and cents to be spent annually (and initially) to provide a house for the client. With the space studies of the three areas under consideration and the general specifications which describe the basic work required to create the desired working environment, you can approach the landlord of the building in which space would be rented or the realtor and builder who would be involved with a new building. The information required covers:

1. For remodeling
(a) The rent per year for net rentable space.
(b) The cost to the client for basic work (including telephone installation charges and professional fees), prorated over the years of the lease.
(c) Total of yearly costs per rentable square foot [(a) plus (b) divided by the number of square feet].

2. For renting
(a) The rent per year for net rentable space.
(b) The cost to the client for basic work (including telephone installation charges, professional fees, and moving costs), prorated over the years of the lease.
(c) Total of yearly costs per rentable square foot [(a) plus (b) divided by number of square feet].

3. For building
The cost of rent plus the cost for building plus the costs of professional fees will be the total cost of the project. One part of this must be an initial investment in the project and can be treated as such or prorated over the years of mortgage retirement. On the assumption that it will be treated as a separate initial investment with the tax advantages of such an investment, the yearly rent should be computed on the basis of:

(a) Interest and amortization per year.
(b) Annual operating and maintenace costs per year.
(c) The cost to the client for basic work (including telephone installation charges, professional fees, and moving costs), prorated over the same number of years of the lease as are being used under (1) and (2).
(d) Total of yearly costs per rentable square foot [(a) plus (b) plus (c) divided by number of square feet].

The conclusions and the recommendations based on these comparisons should be reviewed by financial officers and advisers of the client company, so that they can add their thoughts concerning advantages and disadvantages to the evaluation report.

CHAPTER III EXPLORING

To explore the possible solutions of space layout and the never-ending variety of aesthetic approaches available is to realize the dream of the designer.

The ability to understand the client's operational and aesthetic goals and to imaginatively translate them into the three dimensions of his business home within the framework of the dollars he has to spend is the challenge and excitement of exploration.

The creative impulse that led you to the field of planning and designing in the first place finds its release in delving, digging, fashioning, refashioning, and finally integrating the forms, and colors, and planes that will be the environment for the personnel and for the activities of the client's operation. ■

SECTION I EXPLORING SPACE USE

The layout, or space study, of the client's requirements, done within the confines of the area he is to occupy, is the first opportunity to show your understanding of the problem. To prepare this study you must, of course, have a plan of the area to be studied, and your plan should be as accurate a plan as it is possible to obtain. First studies are often done on the rental plans of new buildings or on the preliminary plans of a hypothetical building when architectural plans are not available. Studies done on such plans should be clearly marked as "preliminary" and should carry a legend pointing out the fact that measurements are not accurate. Before the space study becomes a final study, the plan must be made accurate either by basing it on the final **architectural plans** of the building that is being built or by taking field dimensions on the site of the existing building, if it is possible to do so. If the study and the later **working drawings** are based on the architectural plans of a building being built, the accuracy of these plans should be constantly checked against each issue of newer, later-dated drawings. Also, they should be checked against the construction going on in the building. Constant vigilance is urged because architectural changes can be many as building planning progresses, just as on-the-job changes will continue to be made as construction progresses. Columns have a way of getting bigger; pipes appear where least expected; and major ducts can unexpectedly materialize to play havoc with ceiling heights in areas where height is important.

To understand the steps required in the preparation of a space study, it would be well to follow one through to completion, starting with the client's requirements. To keep the exercise as uncomplicated as possible, a relatively simple business operation will be used. Remember that when you take requirements you must describe the operation as clearly and as completely as you can. Depending upon the size of the design company, it is quite possible that the space study may be prepared by someone in your space-study department who will have to interpret the client's operation from written requirements given to him.

For the exercise the study will be prepared after requirements have been taken and the inventory has been completed. Quite often in actual practice the study may be done before the inventory is taken. This is usually the case when a client, contemplating a move into space he will rent, needs to know as quickly as possible, and without getting involved in too great an expense, whether or not he will fit into that space. When the study is to be done without benefit of inventory, you will have to add to your requirement notes information concerning any concentration of space-taking equipment that you see when touring the client's premises. This would include files, storage cabinets, safes, shelving, etc.

You will note that, even on the rather simple operational requirement form listed below, each department, area, etc., is given an identifying number. This same number would be carried through on all documents, including inventory sheets and tabulation forms. The company whose requirements are being used in the space study exercise will later be used to illustrate other steps in the development of our planning procedures, and the manner in which these numbers are keyed into other forms and drawings will become apparent further on in the text.

OPERATIONAL REQUIREMENTS
ABC Corporation, Sales Division

The ABC Corporation manufactures and sells office machines, such as typewriters and adding machines. This sales-division office (not part of a street-floor showroom) houses both the local sales department and the international sales department. Both are under the sales manager of the company who is also a corporate vice-president. The visitors to these offices are mostly buyers from foreign countries and company officials who meet in the division conference room at least three times weekly.

Identification Number		Locate Near
1.	Reception room—seating for four to five people—table for literature. Control by secretary	2(a)
2.	Open area	
2(a).	Three secretaries Five letter files	1, 4, 5
2(b).	Four salesmen and one secretary Seven letter files	4, 7
3.	Private office—sales manager needs large office with seating for six to seven people—prefers no desk—would like a conference table instead	4, 5, 9
4.	Private office—assistant sales manager—local sales	2(a), 2(b), 3
5.	Private office—assistant sales manager—international sales	2(a), 3, 6
6.	Private office—assistant to five	5
7.	Semiprivate office—three people sales processing—work with 2(b) in handling of sales paper	2(b), 8

Drawing 8

```
                    ┌──────────────────┐
                    │  SALES MGR.  [3] │
                    └──────────────────┘
┌──────────────────┐   ┌──────────┐   ┌──────────────────┐
│ ASS'T SALES MGR. [4]│ │ ASS'T [6]│   │ ASS'T SALES MGR. [5]│
└──────────────────┘   └──────────┘   └──────────────────┘

┌──────────────────┐      ( CONF. RM. )     ┌──────────────────┐
│ SALESMAN AND SEC'Y. [2b]│    [9]          │  SECRETARIES  [2a]│
└──────────────────┘                        └──────────────────┘

┌──────────────────┐      ( STORAGE )        ( RECEPTION )
│ SALES PROCESSING [7]│     [8]                  [1]
└──────────────────┘
```

☐ PERSONNEL AREAS

○ SERVICE AREAS

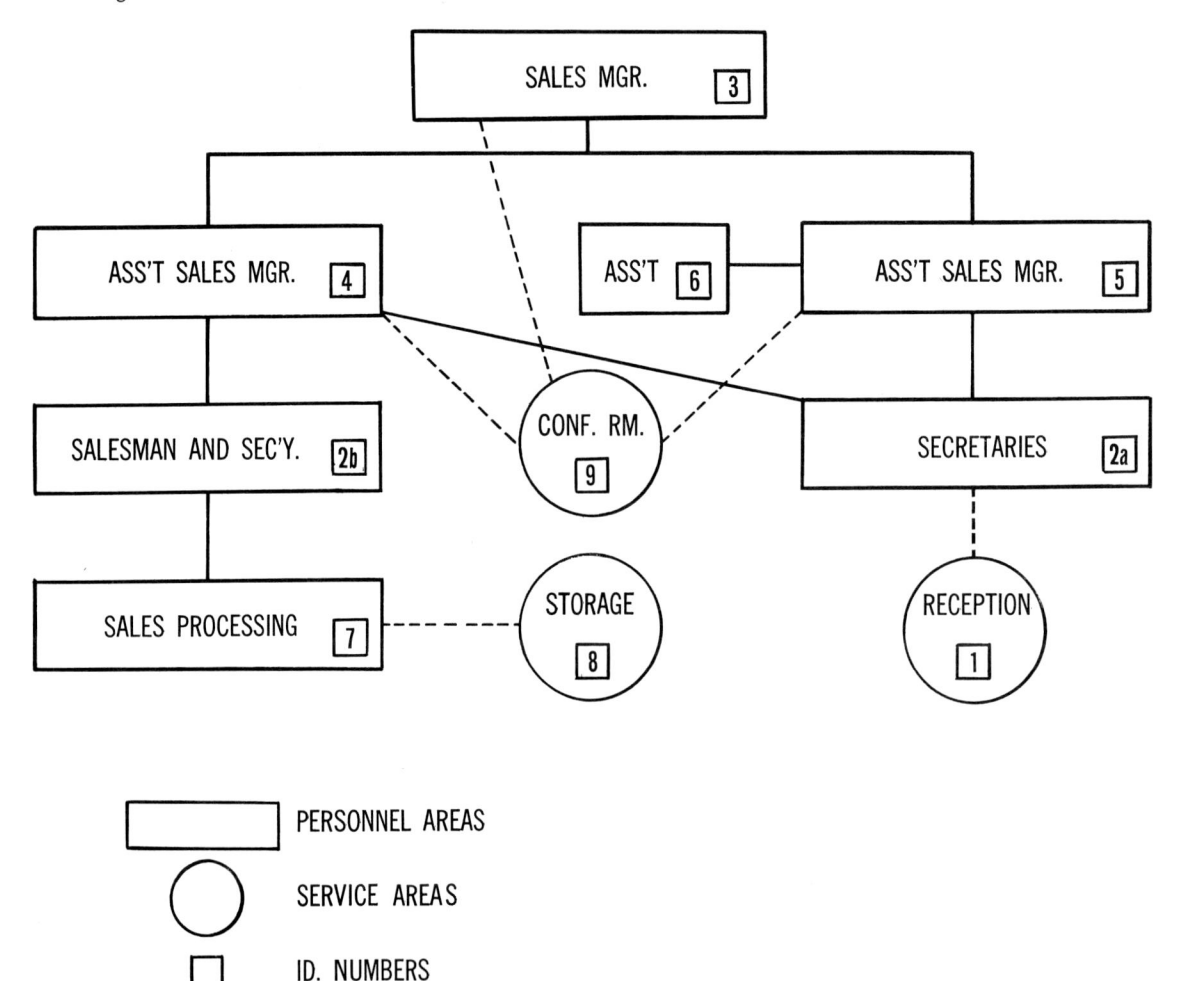

▫ ID. NUMBERS

ORGANIZATION CHART
ABC Corporation, Sales Division

The organization chart illustrates the interrelationships and responsibilities of the personnel of the ABC Corporation. The chain of command is indicated by the solid lines, while the broken lines show the relationship of personnel to service areas. The identification numbers have been taken from the requirement form.

Exploring Space Use 67

8. Storage and reproduction room—used almost exclusively by 7—room is now 100 sq ft—need twice as much space 7
9. Conference room—meeting room—seating for six to seven informally with no conference table—access to galley for coffee making, refrigerator, sink 3, 4, 5

Your next step is to apply footages to the requirements in order to arrive at the amount of space needed to house the operation. Chapter II has already described the manner in which calculations are arrived at when the problem is complex. For a job as simple as this, the operational-requirement form could be used for the inventory and the tabulation as well. However, because most of your jobs will require inventory forms, the inventory and tabulation for this exercise are shown below on the simplified form.

INVENTORY AND FOOTAGE TABULATION
(Simplified Form)
ABC Corporation, Sales Division

Identification Number	Footage Required Sq Ft
1. Reception—four chairs (purchase*), two tables (purchase)	100†
2(a). Secretaries—three 60 × 30 in. desks with 18 × 36 in. L's and one interview chair next to each—each with telephone and electric typewriter. One desk to carry five trunkline monitor board	185
2(b). Salesmen—four 60 × 30 in. desks—each with telephone Secretary—One 60 × 30 in. desk with 18 × 36 in. L Telephone and electric typewriter	280
3. Private office—(purchase) sofa, end table, lounge chair, round conference table for four, four conference chairs, two telephones	320
4. Private office—60 × 30 in. desk, swivel, two pull-up chairs, settee, end table, telephone	160
5. Private office—60 × 30 in. desk, swivel, two pull-up chairs, one 42 in. credenza, telephone	160
6. Private office—60 × 30 in. desk, swivel, two chairs, telephone	100
7. Semiprivate office—four 60 × 30 in. desks with 18 × 36 in. L's, five legal files with storage above—one 60 × 30 in. worktable, one telephone, four typewriters	250
8. Storage—five legal files, Xerox 813, small mail machine on counter—approximately 10 to 15 ft of counter with storage beneath and above	250

(continued)

Drawing 9

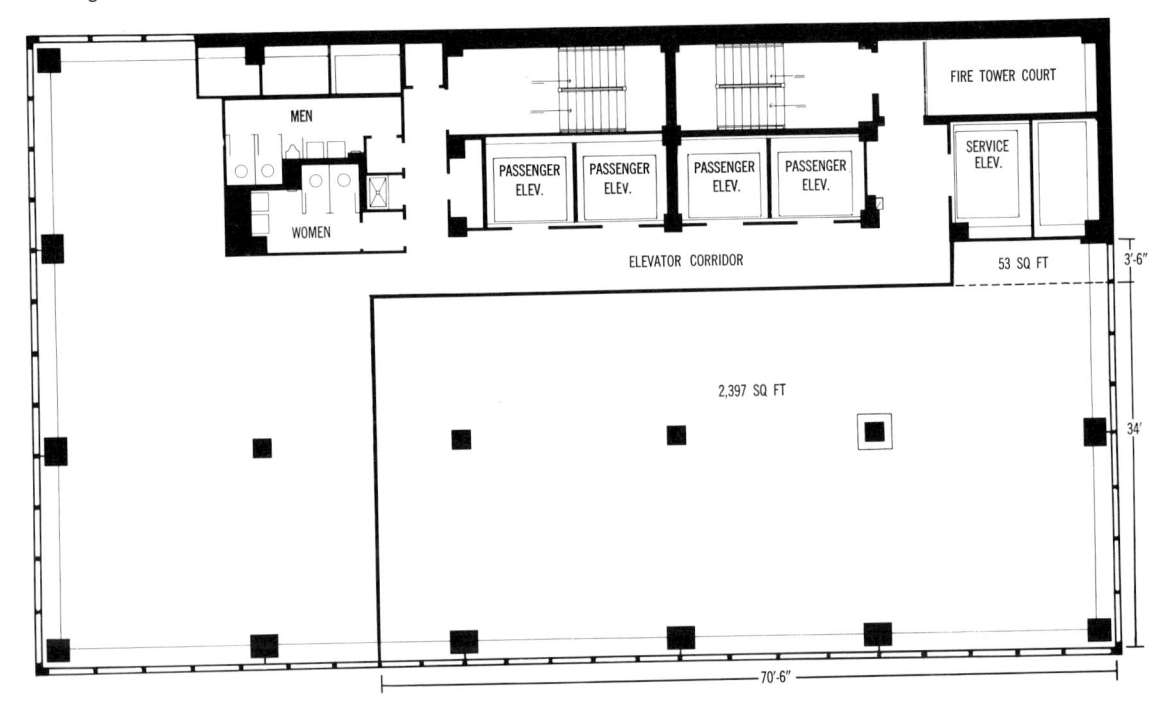

AREA CALCULATIONS

The two shaded areas of this drawing represent the amount of usable space required for the ABC Corporation. (Actually, it provides for 90 square feet more than is needed, but the desirability of maintaining a straight wall between the client's space and the balance of the floor forced this overage.) The usable footage of 2,450 square feet, multiplied by the already established factor (see page 49) of 1.3, brings the total to 3,185 square feet of rentable space.

9. Conference room—sofa, end table, coffee table, four lounge chairs, one small table for telephone (purchase). Galley (purchase). Should be a spacious room   250
                                                                                                                                                    ─────
                                                                                                                                                    2,055
                                                               Add 15% for intradept. traffic   305
                                                                                                 ─────
                                                                                                 2,360

* All furniture is existing, except where indicated for purchase.
† Reception-room footage is arrived at by assigning 20 square feet per person. This can vary greatly, depending upon other requirements of the room, such as display areas. All other sizes are based on job requirements.

The operational requirements, the inventory, and the footage tabulation will be noted on the simple forms just shown or on the many pages of a voluminous report. Prior to translating these requirements into a space study, you must be sure that you understand the interoffice traffic and paper flow. To help grasp this quickly, you can prepare an organization chart. This is a very useful tool for the beginner and an aid even to the most experienced planner in very complicated, large operations. The organization chart that reflects the requirements listed on page 65 is illustrated on Drawing 8.

With the requirements and inventory taken, you are now ready to start your study of the space the client may use. (The preparation of the plan of the floor on which the study is to be done—the **core plan**—and the manner in which core-plan files are kept so that plans are available when required for a space study, is discussed in the second section of Chapter VII).

The space-study exercise is done on the same core as that used on Drawing 9. It will be used throughout to illustrate the many plan steps to be taken in preparing project drawings.

Since the tabulation of client requirements showed a need for less than the full floor, the first step is to create the **public corridors** required on a multiple-tenancy floor. In this building the owner requested that public corridors be 7 feet wide at the elevator bank. This size is very often determined at the discretion of the building owner (who may ask you or his architect for advice in setting the corridor dimension), but it must, in any event, be no narrower than the local building code dictates. With the boundaries of the corridor drawn in, the next step is to block in the area or areas that will give you the number of usable feet needed. First you

Drawing 10

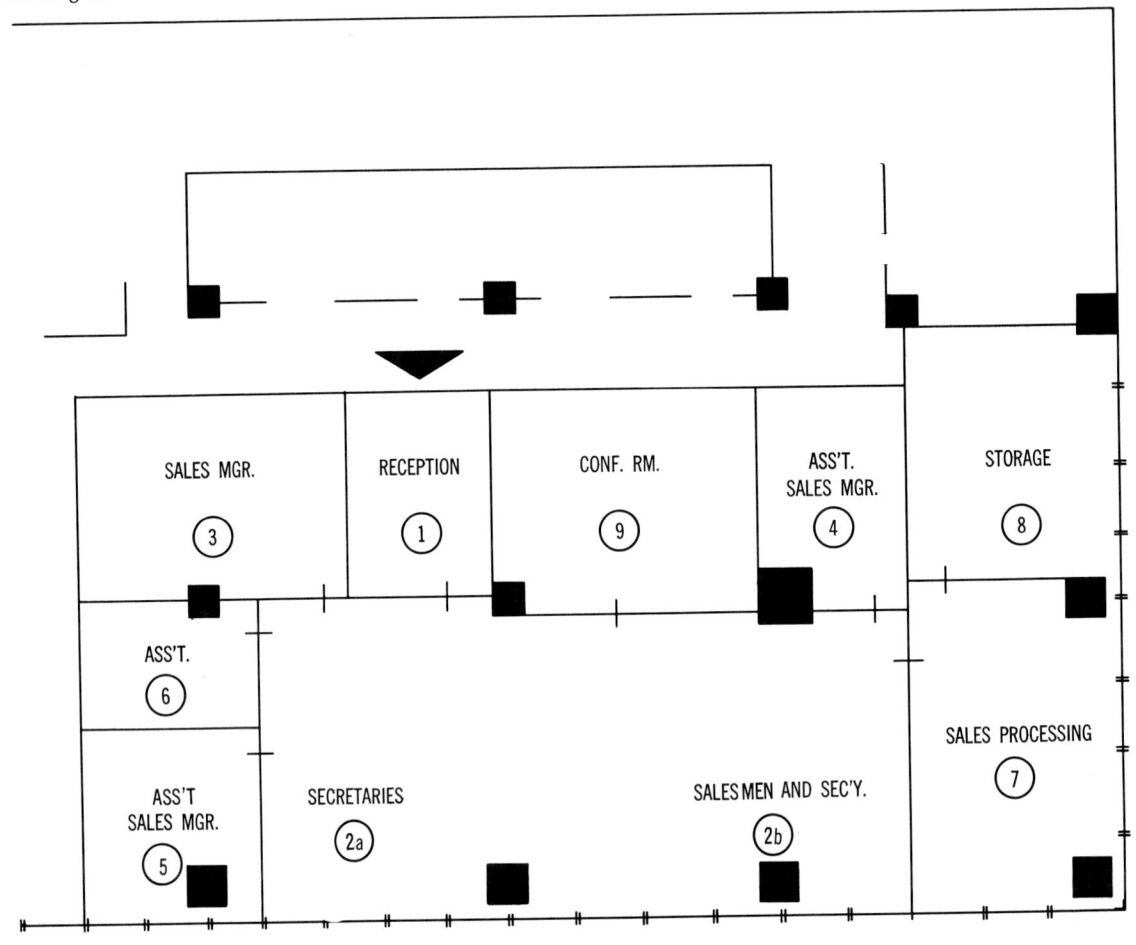

	SALES MGR. ③	RECEPTION ①	CONF. RM. ⑨	ASS'T. SALES MGR. ④	STORAGE ⑧
	ASS'T. ⑥				
	ASS'T. SALES MGR. ⑤	SECRETARIES ②a		SALESMEN AND SEC'Y. ②b	SALES PROCESSING ⑦

SPACE STUDY — ROUGH
ABC Corporation, Sales Division

In this study, an attempt was made to provide one large block of space for all personnel requiring open area and to locate near the windows those people who sit at their desks throughout the day. Although the study accomplishes both desires, it fails to maintain other required relationships. Another undesirable feature of the study is the fact that it places the storage room at windows instead of in interior space.

must decide what part of the floor the client will occupy if such a decision has not already been made by the renting agent or building owner. This decision can be made for one or more of many reasons: position of reception room with relation to the elevators, desirability and availability of the sublet area that would be created, general contour of the space for client's use, etc. Sometimes if there is no other particular reason for the choice, the layout itself may indicate which area on the floor is best for the client's requirements. In this exercise the choice was made based on quickly drawn roughs which indicated the advantages of the area used.

To explore the many solutions possible, your first concern will be to sketch as many basic concepts as you can. Rough sketches prepared on tissue overlays will allow you to produce many schemes rapidly without bogging down with the details that, at this point in your study development, are completely unnecessary. Drawings 10, 11, and 12 are rough studies done within this space illustrating different approaches to the solution of the problem.

Occasionally the study will point up protocol problems unrealized when you took requirements. One company was moving into a building with comparatively little window space—in fact, less window space than they had in their old building—so that all of the private offices could not be placed at windows. The president, informed of the problem, solved it when he took an interior office without windows. Nobody dared complain after that.

Drawing 13 illustrates a finished space study based on the rough study shown on Drawing 12. What should or should not be done on the presented study is discussed in **Checklist G—Space Study.** The space study is prepared primarily to prove to the client that he fits into the space he may rent. The client to whom you show the study and who must understand how well it works (or doesn't work) usually knows little about reading a plan. You must be prepared to interpret it for him and make it as easy as possible for him to judge it. He must be able to follow your interpretation of his requirements, so that there are no surprises for him after the space is built. Relationships that sounded right to the client in the telling very often prove wrong when he sees the actual plan. Rarely does a study stay unchanged but, unless you have completely misunderstood the business operation, the first study should be a good starting point for intelligent

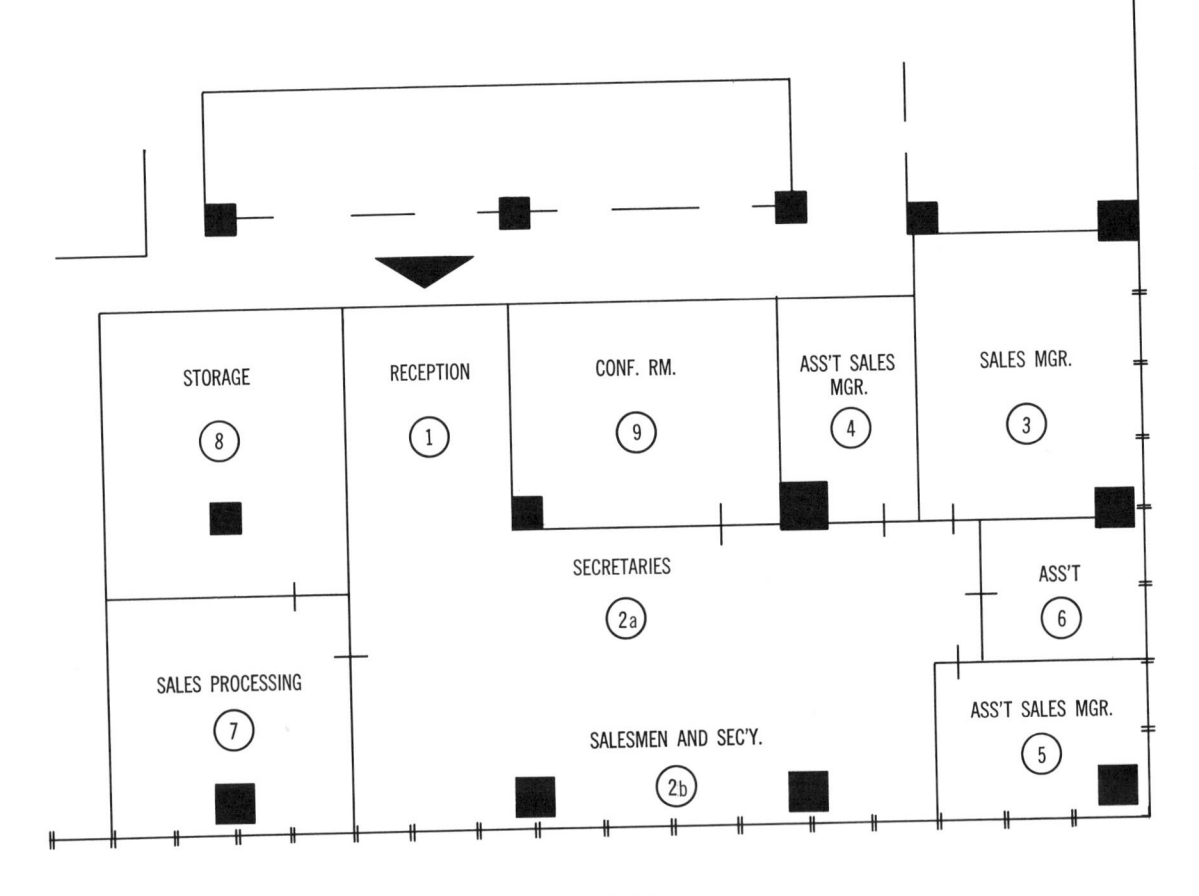

STORAGE (8)	RECEPTION (1)	CONF. RM. (9)	ASS'T SALES MGR. (4)	SALES MGR. (3)

SECRETARIES (2a)

ASS'T (6)

SALES PROCESSING (7)

SALESMEN AND SEC'Y. (2b)

ASS'T SALES MGR. (5)

SPACE STUDY — ROUGH
ABC Corporation, Sales Division

This study revised the position of the private offices, placed the storage room away from the windows, and still managed to provide one large block of open area. However, it fails to meet other required relationships.

refinements that will ultimately translate the client's requirements into efficiently planned space.

SECTION II EXPLORING THE BUDGET

After a space study that satisfies the client's requirements has been completed, the next step is to develop the budgetary framework for all design, construction, and purchasing.

To prepare the budget, you will have to use the information gathered when you reviewed the items on Checklist D—Design and Construction Requirements. Should the client rent his space, you will then include the items covered in the work letter that is normally part of the lease. The work letter is that part of a lease that itemizes the construction work to be supplied and installed for the tenant at no cost to him. It is quite customary for a landlord to supply basic construction for the tenant in both new and old buildings, but sometimes the landlord, to avoid problems of negotiating specifics of work, will give dollars in lieu of the work to be done. At other times, usually when the client is renting space in an older building, the landlord may supply no work at all. In these last two cases there is, of course, no reason for a work letter to be made part of the lease.

When the landlord is giving basic work, the tenant, his lawyer, and his real estate consultant meet to negotiate with the landlord and his attorneys to arrive at lease terms satisfactory to all parties. Quite frequently the tenant's space planner is asked to sit in at the lease-negotiating meetings to discuss and explain items in the work letter. When he does not sit in at the meetings, he may be asked to supply particulars of basic work that could be negotiated for and made part of the work letter.

The ultimate budget depends upon the amount of work the landlord will contribute. Whether or not you leave the preparation of the budget until after the lease has been negotiated depends upon each specific situation. Sometimes the budget, prepared in advance, is used in negotiating, so that the client will know the dollar value of the items that are being discussed; in other instances it will have to be part of the evaluation re-

Drawing 12

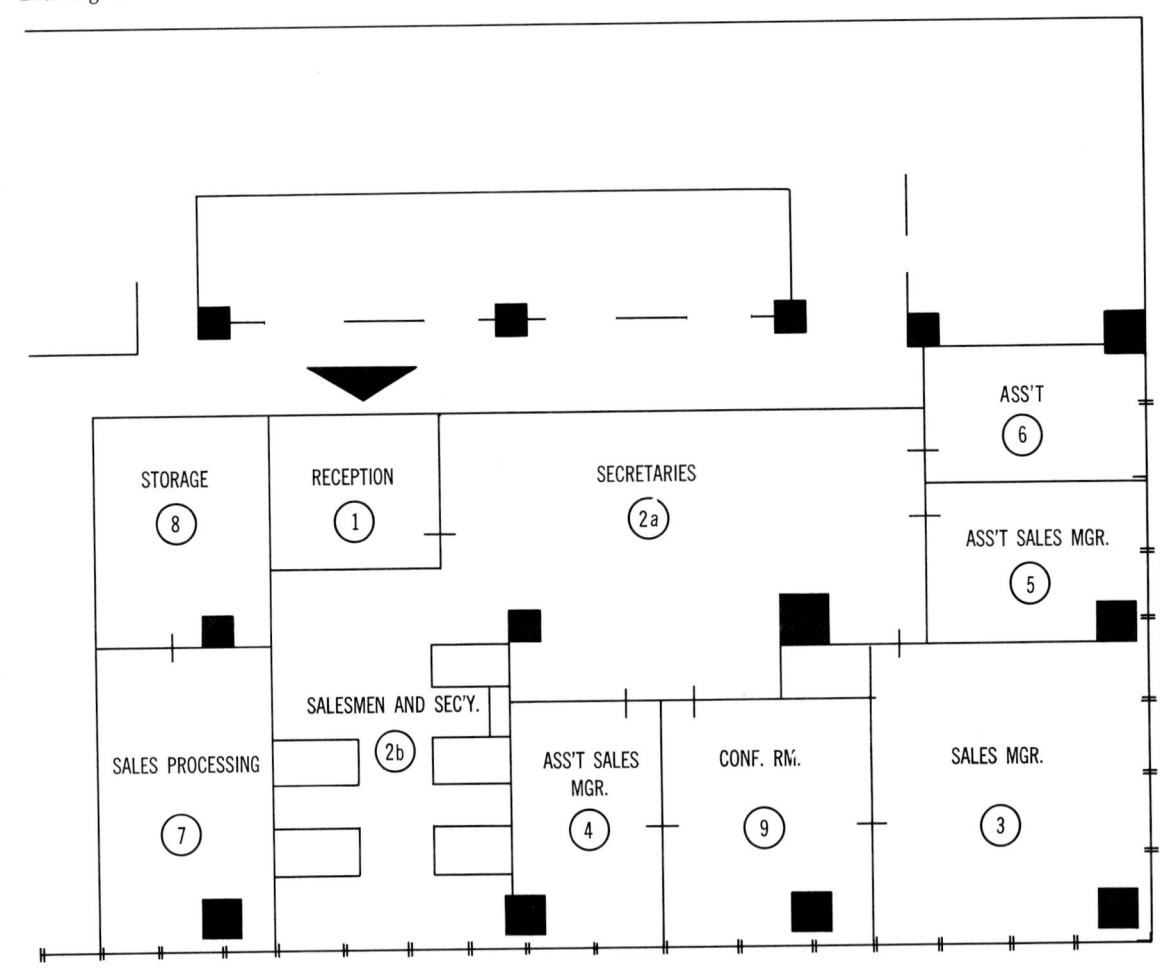

SPACE STUDY — ROUGH
ABC Corporation, Sales Division

This study shows all offices on the periphery of the building, maintains the desirable relationships between offices and services, and logically separates 2a and 2b, placing each closest to those people with whom each works. One particular area (2b) seemed a little small to house the furniture and equipment required for it. The furniture was sketched in to prove the adequacy of the area before proceeding. Do this for your edification, even though you will not show furniture on the space study. You will then know that the furniture actually fits should the client question that fact.

port outlined in Checklist F on page 58. No matter what the chronological order, you will eventually be involved in both the work-letter portion of the lease and in the preparation of the budget of job costs.

Up to now the work letter has been discussed in relation to the work the landlord will do for the tenant. Actually it will cover much more than just the listing of the work itself. **Checklist H** at the end of this chapter is a list of items to be considered in the preparation of the work letter, along with the items on Checklist D.

There are, however, other aspects of the landlord's effort which do not deal with items of work but which should be made part of the work letter.

Practically all leases carry a start-of-rent date tied in with an occupancy date. If it is the landlord's responsibility to do the work for the tenant, his ability to get the tenant into his space by the occupancy date depends upon his getting plans far enough in advance to allow him to do the necessary construction and installation. So the work letter will carry paragraphs that deal with the required delivery dates of the tenant's plans. You will probably be asked to agree or disagree with the dates proposed, and in doing so you must protect the client and make sure that you do not shorten any of the time that may be needed for proper planning and design. Since it is not necessary that all plans be delivered at the same time, it is quite possible to write into the lease as many as four different dates for **plan delivery.** The categories and the order of their required delivery would be:

1. Plans showing location of all floor areas where reinforcing is required (such as file areas, libraries, and telephone-equipment rooms) as well as any areas where floors must be pierced for stairwells, dumbwaiters, etc. These plans should be delivered first in case they require work on the part of the **structural engineer** of the building.

2. Plans showing location, specifications, and distribution of lighting fixtures, plumbing, heating and ventilating controls, room occupancy, heat-producing equipment, and any other factors pertinent to the preparation of **mechanical engineering** plans, to be done by the landlord's or tenant's engineers.

3. The working drawings and specifications for work to be done.

4. Drawings and specifications covering the finishing work, including flooring, wall covering, paint and decorative treatments, and locations of cabinetwork.

SPACE STUDY
ABC Corporation, Sales Division

This refinement of the rough study of Drawing 12 is prepared for presentation to the client. Each room is marked with its identification number taken from the original requirements. Room sizes are shown, and although their showing is a matter of designer discretion, this study includes titles of occupants, names of service areas, clothes closets, drinking fountain, and the galley required for the conference room. The study must illustrate the relationships of the organization as you see them. They must be so depicted as to be crystal clear to the client.

Drawing 13

Engineering plans mentioned in (2) above are usually prepared by the engineers who designed the building system, in order to assure an efficient air-conditioning installation. There would be no single responsibility for the functioning of the air-conditioning system (or anything else in the building) if each tenant brought in his own engineer.

If the building is not an air-conditioned building and the system to be installed is for the client's use only, the air-conditioning engineer can be retained by the landlord or by the tenant. This would depend upon whether the landlord or tenant is contractually responsible for the performance and maintenance of the system.

The cost of reinforcing floor areas that require it is an item that must be negotiated and made part of the work letter.

The work-letter portion of the lease should spell out the right of the tenant to use contractors of his own choice for some of the finishing-trades work such as carpentry, millwork, cabinetwork, wall covering, carpeting, and draperies. The lease should give these trades the right to work in the premises without interfering with, or interference from, the landlord's contractors, and with sufficient time to finish their work before tenant occupancy.

The lease must provide for the help that the client will have to get when he moves into the space. Should the move take place at night (and most moves do), elevator service, light, power, air conditioning, and porter service would be required.

The work letter should also give the tenant the right to substitute materials for the building-standard materials being furnished and installed for him by the landlord. The tenant must, of course, pay for any overage in costs. He should be given a credit for substituted materials, and it would be well, to avoid later disputes, if the work letter were to contain a list of dollar credits available against the substituted items.

The items for which substitutes are most often chosen include flooring, partitions, doors, hardware, lighting fixtures, and wall painting or wall covering. Although the tenant should get credit for substituted material, he should not expect to get a credit for any item or items that are eliminated from the plans, even though they were offered in the work letter.

Very often the landlord will have to install more of a particular item than the work letter allows. This would then be an extra cost to the tenant.

When possible, the lease should carry the dollar costs that would be charged for such standard, extra items. These could include the cost of supplying and installing electrical outlets, telephone outlets, switches, lighting fixtures, and any of the other items on Checklists D and H.

To avoid any problems of delay in construction, the work letter should establish a limit of days for the approval or disapproval of tenant extra costs. These are the extra costs or bids, covering extra work or substitute work, that are to be paid for by the tenant. The costs for these items must be submitted to the tenant for his written approval before any of the work should be done.

The budget should be presented to the client before you begin your design effort. The items it contains will have been arrived at as a result of the discussions described in Chapter I concerning aesthetic goals and financial limitations. The purpose of the budget presentation is to detail the costs of all of the things the client needs, of all the things he thinks he wants, and of all the things you think he should have. Although much of the discussion at the design meeting may deal in generalizations, the budget will have to be as detailed and as specific as possible. It should not, for example, show a lump sum of $10,000 as the cost for building and furnishing the reception room. It should instead show that this total is the sum of the costs for electrical, air conditioning, floor covering, partitions, doors, ceilings, cabinetwork, furniture and furnishings, etc. Much of this breakdown, and in particular the costs of furniture, furnishings, wall covering, carpeting, and cabinetwork, will have to be based on educated guesses arrived at through your interpretation of client needs discussed with him at the design meeting. These guesses will become more and more educated as you gain more and more exposure to design problems.

First budgets generally go through client revision, and a second budget will probably be presented before you begin your design work. The budget presented for the third time will reflect actual prices on those items selected for the presentation that can be specified for purchase. It will still be in the "guesstimate" stage for those things, such as cabinetwork, which would have to be bid on after further details have been prepared.

The items to be priced will come from Checklist D—Design and Construction Requirements, and the work letter will serve as a check for spotting items to be done by the landlord and those items that would be extra costs. It would also reflect the credits to be given where substitute materials are to be used.

The actual pricing of items to be included in the budget is no more complicated than are the normal procedures for **job estimating.** Quantities must be detailed in terms of measurement units such as number, square feet, linear feet, and weight. Cost information by unit of measurement should be gathered and collated, and prevailing trade prices constantly updated in order to assure accurate budgeting. The information should be gathered from contractors, subcontractors, catalog price lists, and all available sources of supply. Differences in prices in different localities should be carefully checked whenever the work is being done in geographical sections in which you have done no previous jobs.

The preparation of the budget, requiring attention to many details, should start with its physical form. Here again each designer will create the form that best suits his particular needs, and he should keep in mind several facts that may influence its design:

1. Each budget will probably be revised at least three times. It should be made as easy as possible for the client to compare prices and items in each of the revisions.

2. A clear, detailed budget can serve a secondary function as a cost-control form for the client and you.

3. The budget form should be designed so that you can clearly see the total cost of all trades for each area of space—private offices, reception room, accounting department, etc.

Presenting the preliminary budget to the client is an experience of its own. During the initial discussion of financial limitations, possible job costs should have been thoroughly analyzed and discussed, so that there would be no particular surprise or shock when the budget is presented. Very often, when costs are first discussed, the question is asked about a rule-of-thumb figure that can be used to determine what an office installation should cost. Actually there is no such rule. The move of two tenants into the same building illustrates this fact very vividly. Both received the same basic work from their landlord—work spelled out in their leases. One, who rented 10,000 square feet of space, was determined to spend nothing above what the landlord was to give him, except for moving costs and telephone installation. At the last minute he decided to spend $835 for a new sofa in his reception room and a wall of flexwood in the same room. The other client, renting 70,000 square feet of space, spent about 75 cents per square foot in 62,000 square feet of work area in his space. In the remaining 8,000 square feet of executive and showroom area, he spent over $600,000.

No, there is no rule of thumb, and the very lack of it emphasizes the importance of the design meeting and the budget that it helps to prepare. Clients with no idea of construction and furnishing costs must be helped at the very beginning of a job to determine just where their available dollars can and should be allocated.

The reaction of clients to the budget varies considerably. One type of client is prepared to come to grips with the problem immediately, by accepting, rejecting, adding, or subtracting before the meeting ends. Other clients will want several days to study the budget and to discuss it with others in their company before making a decision. Still others will want all the items listed on the budget, but for less money. This can be accomplished sometimes by specifying less expensive elements (not always acceptable to the client), but sometimes it can't be done at all. The end result of the budget meeting and the budget study is that finally a budget is established, the client knows what he is to get for his money, and you have the financial guidelines for your next step—design.

SECTION III   EXPLORING DESIGN

The details of design exploration cannot really be started until you have honestly faced the broader aspects of your own design thinking. Although this is a textbook on office planning and design and not a treatise on design philosophy (and certainly not a personal essay on the author's philosophy), you should spend a moment thinking about your design goals. What role do you as designers expect to play in planning the future? Will you truly plan it, or will you merely be the technician who does the working drawings for an evolutionary design that will take place despite you? Faced with the day-to-day problems of office design, do you design what you want or do you give the client what he wants?

There is no one answer. Each of you must find his own way to his own answer through his own exposure to design problems. Offices have been designed completely as the designer demanded that they be designed, and the client loved them. Offices have been designed completely as the designer demanded they be designed, and the client hated them. Offices have been designed the way the client wanted them designed, and the designer hated them.

We believe that the designer is the planner of the future—the leader but not the dictator. The dictator theory works no better in creative fields than it does in politics. Our cultural growth comes from education through exposure to books, not from book burning.

An important part of the designer's role is to elevate, not dictate. By attempting to arbitrarily impose his will, the designer adds nothing to the client's understanding or appreciation of design. Design strives to create a better environment for man, but environment can serve its true function of making man a better human being only if man is made to understand his environment. Naturally the best teacher should be the designer himself. If he fails to teach, he fails to fulfill his role.

It is always such a great temptation, particularly on the part of the uninitiated, to set the whole subject of design on a plateau of its own, unrelated to the workaday efforts of plumbers, plasterers, and handymen. But it is not an entity; it is indeed part and parcel of every trade that contributes to it and every step of understanding, analyzing, and exploring from which it springs. If your design effort does not begin with a study of space use based on your understanding of the business to be housed and on the financial limitations that must control the work to be done, the end result of your effort will not successfully contribute to the functional and aesthetic goals of the client.

One reception room planned and designed to house the activities that go on within its walls may be more ornate than another, but, properly planned and properly designed, each detail in each of the rooms will have been chosen for a logical purpose. The high level of lighting intensity in a room used by accountants has the same functional and aesthetic validity

Drawings 14a–c

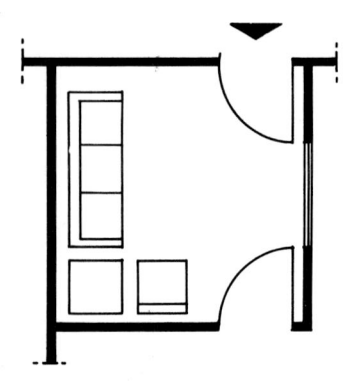

Plan A. Indicates a sofa large enough for three people and an individual lounge chair.

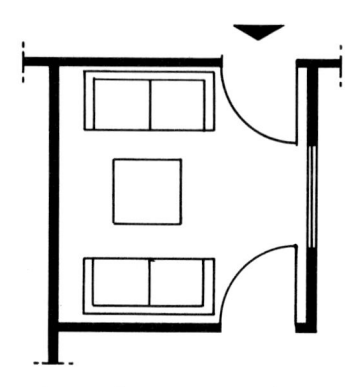

Plan B. Shows a more cohesive arrangement of furniture with a better balance of room area.

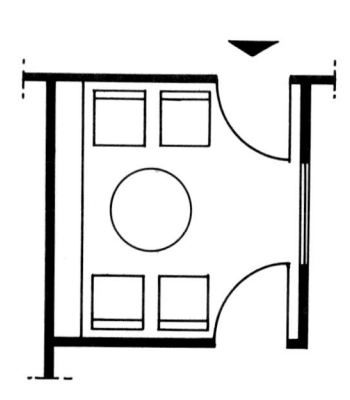

Plan C. Utilizes the advantages of the Plan B layout but substitutes two chairs for each of the two-seater settees. A shelf has been added along the left wall to carry additional literature, a plant, or an art object.

FURNITURE PLANS — DEVELOPMENTAL
Reception Room — ABC Corporation, Sales Division

The three plans show developmental studies for furniture placement within the reception room of the ABC Corporation. Each contains the same number of seats, and each meets the requirements for the room. The sliding glass window in the wall to the right will make it possible to communicate with the secretary-receptionist.

as does the warmth of low-level lighting in a judge's chamber. Each element of design, both the accountant's lighting and the judge's, should be arrived at as the design answer to an occupational problem—the accountant's lighting for the sake of seeing and the judge's lighting for its contribution to creating the atmosphere necessary for the free, quiet interchange of thought.

It is not easy to arrive at an honest answer to an environmental solution of the client's functional problems. It takes work—probing, searching, preparing sketch upon sketch, and making certain that every possible answer has been scrutinized—before you can be satisfied that you have arrived at the best possible solution.

It takes the scrutiny of a plan and the study of all the possible locations of the furniture, furnishings, and other required elements, before you can be certain that everything is where it should be to make the room work as it must.

The three plans of Drawing 14 show studies of possible furniture locations for the reception room as it was defined on the space study, Drawing 13. Even though the last plan of the three, Plan C, seemed to be the best solution, further design exploration brought about changes that resulted in the more open plan illustrated on page 92 as part of the **design presentation.**

With the plan developed you can now begin to review the other elements of design and function—the lighting, the ceiling, the doors, walls and floors, materials, and finishes—as well as the specific furniture and furnishings. The planes and shapes and forms that will help delineate your design answer will come from the many sketches that will be part of the probing and searching for the proper approach to your desired solution. The shuffling and reshuffling may force you to rework the plan developed in the first step of plan study, and this reworking may have to be done again as you examine the third area of search—color, and its impact on total design. This step, too, must go through the same kind of intensive study before you can and should be satisfied that you have found the answer.

Part of your probing and searching must include the constant checking and rechecking of possible design solutions against the dollars allotted to them in the budget. Is there enough money in the budget for this particular room to allow the use of teak panelling or do you borrow the money from another area in order to pay for it? Or do you abandon teak entirely and find a less expensive solution? Design exploration must be done with constant awareness of the financial framework set up by the budget.

Good design is, of course, not measured by the amount of money expended. Very often the intelligent use of building-standard items can result in fine design solutions at no cost to the client. Standard lighting fixtures run at right angles to the length of a corridor rather than parallel to it can, at no extra cost, give the corridor a shorter, wider look. Columns in large open areas, treated colorfully with building-standard paint and contrasted to the walls of the surrounding area, can add a welcome visual relief to the room without adding to the client's expenditure. This kind of creative design thinking can give more latitude to the use of your budgeted dollars.

One of the methods found helpful in the intensive study you must go through in all three of the design steps is the use of the quick sketch, which shows nothing but essential details until plan, elevation, mass, and color balance have been completed. Start with the quick sketch, and refine details after you are on the road to a basic solution. You will then be inclined to do more exploring than if each probing approach involved hours of effort over nonessential details that will probably be scrapped before you can find the answer, anyway. The quick sketch is particularly helpful in exploring color use. An outline sketch of the solution, reproduced as many times as you wish on a copying machine, can be used for rapid color exercises and quick evaluation of color impact on the design theme.

Color in the office, by the way, is no longer confined to the pale green that was so universally used because of its restful quality. The change came about because it finally dawned on someone that offices were for work, not for sleep. Color, as a major contributor to environment, provides its own visual relief by giving the eye interesting new things to look at as heads are raised from work.

The selection of furniture and equipment, integrated with the design of the total space, must also be concerned with the question of standardization. Certainly the purchasing program, should it be a long-range one, will be more effectively accomplished if there is some assurance that the items selected will be readily available as they are needed. In the consideration of office design, thought must be given to the advantages or disadvantages of including some of the elements that may possibly be requested in the design of particular rooms. In the plan studies of Drawing 14, the examination of the seating problem resulted in discarding sofas and loveseats. This is the kind of scrutiny that each element of design should get. As another example, display, requested by many clients, should be studied very carefully before its use is decided upon. As a rule, a display would be set up in a reception room, corridors, conference room, or showroom. There is no element of design that can make an area look dated more rapidly than an untended, unchanged display. Unless the client is prepared to change the display periodically and assign the responsibility for making the changes, the use of display should be discouraged.

The use of clocks in the reception room is a dangerous practice. They tend to remind the visitor that he has been waiting a long time to see someone who promised to "be right out." In fact, clocks anywhere within an office, except where they are specifically needed for operational timing purposes, are not desirable pieces of equipment. In salesrooms and private offices they tend to speed people on their way when your client may not want them to leave. (And you can certainly leave it up to the ingenuity of the client to get rid of the undesirable guest without a clock.)

The facilities for visitor telephones—including the kinds to be used and their placement—are functional elements whose design needs careful study. A service reception area visited by messenger boys who may have to get instructions from their own offices may have a coinbox phone that would be an insult to an executive visitor. The extra phone facility in a conference room can be on the conference table or on a small table in a corner or (to avoid interfering with a meeting in session) in a small telephone room adjacent to the conference room. This, too, is a decision to be made only after careful study of the reasons for the facility and the way in which people will use it.

In addition to your concern with items of this type, you should play a part in the selection and placement of all the finishing touches of the design job—wall decorations, pictures, pieces of sculpture, ashtrays, plants, etc. Your involvement with this part of the project can be as complete or as peripheral as you and your client may want, ranging from the initial selection of the furnishings to the preparation of a manual spelling out what can be used, how and where it can be used, and how it should be cared for. It is well, for example, to set up rules concerning what may be hung on the walls of the client's new offices, because it can be most annoying to see a cartoon from the last issue of the *New Yorker* scotch-taped to the newly painted wall of the stenographer's room. One of the concomitants of space planning and design is to make it possible for people to work together better, but rule making should not be carried too far. In fact, "rules and regulations" provide an ideal opportunity to expose all of the personnel of the client's office to a better understanding of environment and design's contribution to it.

CHECKLIST G SPACE STUDY

The space study is the first visual evidence that the physical area provided by a specific building can adequately contain the client's needs. It must clearly illustrate to him whether he does or does not fit into the space he is considering. It must clearly illustrate how well you have understood his operation, and what economies and efficiencies you are able to bring to it. Since the client in the majority of cases has had little exposure to plan reading, the drawing must be made easy to understand. The following suggestions will help to accomplish this desired clarity:

1. The study should show no furniture. You must know that the furniture and equipment will fit into the space allotted to it (as Drawing 12 shows, you will even sketch it out on the roughs to prove that it does fit), but drawing it on the plan only brings an unnecessarily confusing element into the study. Some planners believe that a study dressed up with furniture and flooring and wood-grained tabletops helps to sell the study. Often it does just the opposite. The prime concern of the client at this point should be the workability of the space—not the details of flowerpot placement.

2. Each area should be clearly marked so that departments and room delineations are easily seen. Whether or not names and titles should be shown should be left up to management, who may, at this early stage, prefer to avoid the jealousies of premature office assign-

ments. If possible, areas should be keyed to the numbers on the operational requirement report.

3. Room dimensions should be shown as width by length. Open areas not rectangular in shape can be dimensioned by a square-foot measurement.

4. The study should carry a legend indicating the number of rentable square feet of the plan.

5. If no field check has been made, the study should carry a legend indicating that the plan was done from a rental or architectural plan and has not been verified in the field.

6. Door openings should be shown for each room.

7. Some planners like to show closets and water coolers on studies, but this is completely discretionary.

8. Neatness and clarity are of the utmost importance. The study must look as well organized as the client wants his company to be.

CHECKLIST H WORK LETTER

The work letter is a document used only when the client is renting space in a building where the landlord supplies work under the terms of the lease. A complete work-letter checklist comes from a combination of the list below, the items on Checklist D—Design and Construction Requirements, and pages 73 to 80, dealing with exploring the budget. Checklist D itemizes those things that can be building-standard, substituted for standard, or used in addition to the standards being supplied. The landlord should make available the specifications for each of the building-standard items being supplied. If, during negotiation, the landlord agrees to supply any non-building-standard items, each should then be written into the work letter. The checklist below contains the details of construction or installation that the landlord may be asked to do, but it is not concerned with the specifications of the items themselves.

1. **Partitions**

    For acoustical purposes, sound baffling above partitions between the slab of the floor above and the hung ceiling, and sound baffling between rooms in the peripheral air-conditioning enclosure

2. **Doors**
   Doors undercut in carpeted areas
3. **Ceilings**
   Plaster all vertical breaks at ceiling height changes
   Venetian blind and drapery pockets recessed at the heads of all windows
4. **Flooring**
   Reducing strip between carpeted and noncarpeted areas
5. **Lighting**
   Fixtures should be provided for by number of fixtures per x number of square feet or by footcandle output of maintained light
   Tubes and lamps for fixtures
6. **Electrical**
   Floor outlets
   Separate circuiting of special outlets
7. **Telephones**
   Floor outlets
   Empty conduits and standard terminal-strip cabinets
8. **Plumbing**
   Rough plumbing and connection of water coolers, sinks, etc.
9. **Heating, Ventilating, and Air Conditioning**
   Work letter should spell out the performance specifications of the system as set up by the building engineers
   Special smoke exhausts, private toilets and kitchen exhausts, thermostatic controls, reheat coils, humidity requirements, and electric-switch controls
   Additional peripheral air-conditioning units by reason of location of tenant's partitions
   Additional regulating valves and thermostats for peripheral private offices
   Acoustical transfer ducts
10. **Painting and Wall Covering**
    Color breaks
    Paint touch-up after tenant moves in

CHAPTER IV   PREPARING

One of the more rewarding aspects of design will come when you prepare and present to the client the drawings, renderings, samples, photographs, and other pertinent details necessary to illustrate your design approach. This is the point in your effort when you will give dimension to your already proven understanding of the client's functional requirements and add to it the form and color of his image.

This is always an exciting time for the designer, no matter how often he goes through these presentations. The anticipation of client reaction and the interest in hearing it voiced equal the ever-recurring anticipation of "opening night."

After the presentation has been approved, a chain reaction is let loose. It starts with the preparation of the working drawings used by contractors for bidding and building and ends with the activation of a purchasing program that will assure the delivery of all the things needed to make the client's offices work as you planned they should. ■

SECTION I   PREPARING A DESIGN PRESENTATION

A **design presentation** has but one reason for being—the necessity to delineate for the client exactly what you are trying to accomplish for him in the plan and design of his space. Each presentation combines a pictorial submission with a financial evaluation of the costs involved.

The financial evaluation is no more nor less than your budget brought up to date. It now includes the specifics of the costs of furniture and fabric, and other details of selection and specification to which actual prices can be assigned. It will also include the updating of your original "guesstimates" on cabinetwork and the other aspects of design that are more detailed now than they were when the first budget was prepared. If, during the exploration of design, you constantly keep the approved budget in mind, your design presentation budget should contain no unhappy surprises for the client.

The pictorial part of the presentation should be as detailed as you can possibly make it and must always be prepared so that the viewer, knowing nothing whatsoever about the subject of office design, can be made to understand exactly what is planned for him. **Checklist I—Design Presentation,** itemizing the "musts" for each submission, is appended to this chapter on page 110.

Just as each designer will want to plan the format of his reports and charts, so too will he want to create the form of his design presentation. However, to show clearly some of the elements that should be part of each presentation a **design plan** (Drawing 15), a **perspective rendering** (Drawing 16), and a **design board** (Drawing 17) were prepared to illustrate part of the design presentation for the ABC Corporation, the company whose requirements are being used as project examples in this text.

The design plan, usually done on a scale larger than that used for the working drawings and the other plans of the project, delineates the furniture, flooring, and accessories in more detail than would be used for a regular furniture plan. The illustrated plan shows details of wood, fabric, flooring, plants, etc. Some design plans are done in color with an indication of wood color, fabric color and weave, carpet color, etc. The purpose of the plan is to clarify the perspective rendering of the room and augment the information that both the rendering and the paste-up board are meant to give the client.

The perspective rendering is the picture that must do the big job of showing the client exactly what it is you are trying to accomplish within the room. Like all such pictorial representations, it can be as detailed or as atmospherically abstract as you wish to make it or as you wish it to be made to get the message to the client. This, too, is part of the design philosophy that must be decided by each designer according to his own particular desires. Drawings in which rooms are made to look twice as large as they really are, with sofas made to look 10 feet long when they are actually 7 feet long, may be fine selling tools for some designers, but others prefer a more exact representation of things as they really are or as close to reality as they can be made to look. The surprise of not getting all that the presentation led him to suspect he was to get can be most unpleasant for the client—and the designer. Even the designers who want everything to be pictured as it will be are forced, in the interest of clarity, to stretch a point or two in the preparation of their drawings. In Drawing 16, for example, the rendering is as close to scale as possible, but still the view is a false one with one wall torn down so that the room can be seen in as wide a perspective as possible.

The third part of the pictorial presentation, the design board, consists of the photographs of furniture and accessories; the samples of carpet, floor tiles, upholstery fabrics, drapery fabrics, leathers, wall covering, wall finishes, and laminates; paint-color swatches; and all other samples that represent the selected materials shown on the perspective rendering. In addition to showing photographs of the furniture, it would be well to get the client to see and to try the furniture you are suggesting for him. His desk chair should certainly be "tried on for size." Each client has such personal sitting habits that it would be well to make certain that the chair is right for him. Occasionally, when it is impossible for the client to visit showrooms, the furniture supplier may be able to send a sample of the chair to the client for a "try-on." One way or another, you should try to get the client and his people to see the furniture they will use. Not everyone is capable of understanding exactly what furniture is like when he sees it in photographs. Seeing and trying the actual pieces will avoid any later disappointment.

Shopping with the client has its dangers as well as its advantages. A

Drawing 15

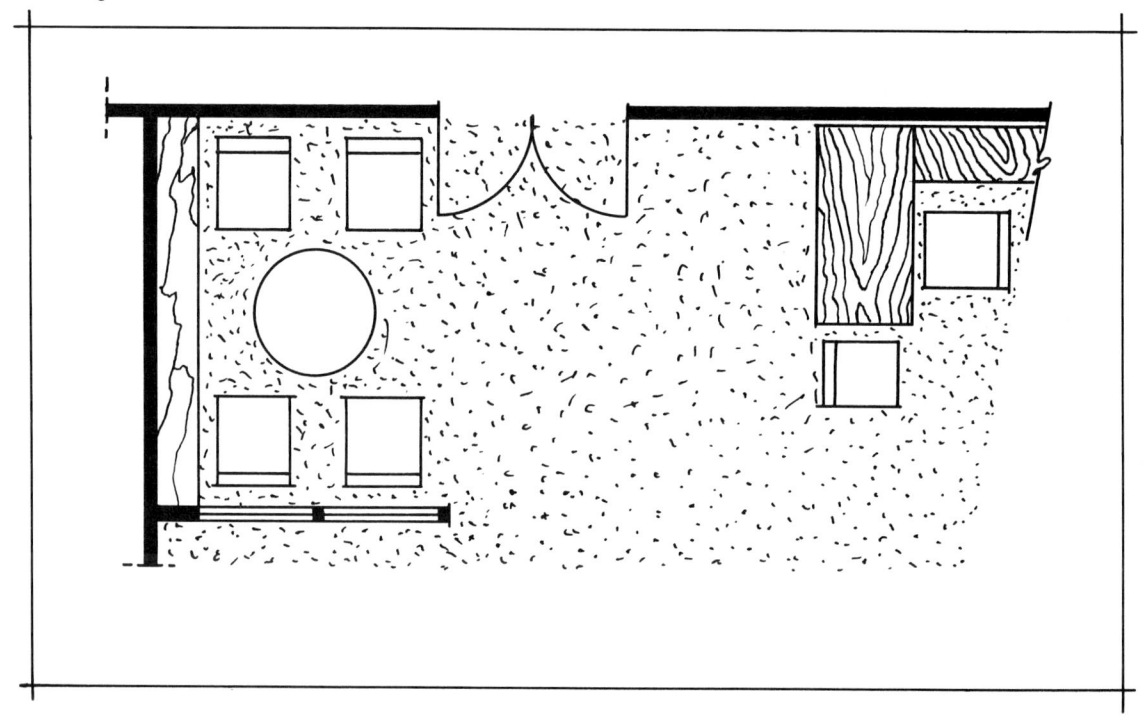

DESIGN PRESENTATION — DESIGN PLAN
Reception Room — ABC Corporation, Sales Division

This is a design refinement of the furniture plan shown on Drawing 14c. Further study of the area and of the requirements for the reception room led to the open plan attained by the removal of the side wall and the introduction of a double-door entrance. The glass dividing wall backed by planters gives definition to the room but still helps to retain the openness that gives a more spacious appearance to the area. The shelf remains as do all the other pieces of furniture.

client wandering around a showroom suddenly becomes exposed to things other than those that have been suggested. As a result you may spend more time with the client than you had anticipated, as you explain the reasons for the choices that have been made.

The drawings shown illustrate a presentation for a specific project. Not all presentations will be alike. The furniture plan can be of a room, a part of the space being planned, or the entire space, depending upon the size of the project and the extent of the design within the project. The perspective renderings can be finished drawings, quick sketches, in color, black-and-white perspectives, or simply elevations of specific areas such as cabinet walls.

Sometimes management will decide that a group of executives, such as account executives in an advertising agency or associates in a law or accounting office, should have the same kind and amount of furniture. Each would then be given a choice of colors and fabrics, and a rendering would be prepared of the typical room. Three or four design boards would then show the available alternate color and fabric schemes.

The design boards can be boards; they can be prepared in book form; they can be prepared as cover flaps for the renderings; or in one of a dozen other presentation methods. Again, each designer will devise his own way to present design, but each must remember that no matter how creative or clever his presentation form may be, its prime purpose is to make his design thinking clear to the client.

Not all rooms will warrant the preparation of either perspective or elevation drawings. In fact, many areas within the spaces you are designing will be shown in much simpler fashion. Design plans, accompanied by design boards showing the details of photographs and samples, will be all that will be needed for many of the private offices, secretarial corridors, open areas, or service areas. In other areas, not included on any of the design-presentation material already described, the disposition of wall and floor finishes and colors will have to be indicated and illustrated through floor plans showing paint and color specifications, plus design boards showing material samples.

Although the form of the presentation is extremely important, it is also important to plan for the way in which presentation will be made and

DESIGN PRESENTATION — PERSPECTIVE RENDERING
Reception Room — ABC Corporation, Sales Division

A view of the reception room and secretarial area. The wall that has been "removed" for the sake of the drawing is the corridor wall opposite the elevators. The arrow indicates the position of the entrance doors.

Drawing 16

Preparing   95
a Design
Presentation

where it will be made. This is not so much a matter of "selling," but rather one of understanding the importance of the presentation for both client and designer.

At the presentation you will be asking the client to make decisions that will affect not only what his offices will look like, but the spending of the money necessary to make them look that way. You should have and he should want to give his undivided attention to what is really his problem.

In actual practice, you will find it advisable to hold the presentations in your own offices. The client should be asked not to have his office call him and you, of course, should take no calls of your own during a presentation. Also, by having the presentation in the designer's office, it is possible to have alternate samples of colors, materials, furniture, etc., brought in immediately should substitutes be necessary. This can appreciably cut down on decision-making time by avoiding the necessity of coming back to the client days later and having to go through a reorientation with him in order to select an alternate color for a storage-room wall.

The presentation should be carefully conducted, with one room or area shown at a time. It would be best to complete the entire presentation before inviting comments or questions about details. The client should see the total concept before he begins to concern himself with the details of any one room. Very often the questions that beset him at the beginning will get answered before the presentation has been concluded.

The way in which the client accepts or rejects the design presentation is predictable only to the extent that he will fall into one of two basic categories: the decision maker or the decision leaner. The first says "yes" or "no" or "yes with changes." The second needs time to make the decision and will, admittedly or without informing you, lean on his wife, secretary, decorator, associate, or friend for his decisions.

The client who said, after seeing a design presentation, "This is not my preconceived idea of what my offices would look like. I retained you to design them because I had faith in your ability, so please carry them out just this way," comes close to being the perfect client.

It is the "leaner" who causes the most serious problems for himself and for the dedicated designer whose presentation is the result of weeks and months of background study of the client's problems, plus years of training and exposure to hundreds of such problems. To be suddenly faced

Drawing 17

DESIGN BOARD A   ABC CORPORATION

DESIGN PRESENTATION — DESIGN BOARD
Reception Room — ABC Corporation, Sales Division

The design board shows the details of the perspective rendering, Drawing 16. On it are mounted photographs of chairs, tables, desks, and planters and samples of woods, fabrics, and flooring. The purpose of the board is to clarify the rendering, and it should show as complete a sampling of the details as is possible.

with the taste of wife or secretary (who, because she has been asked, must voice a criticism) will try the tact, the patience, and the nerves of any designer who allows this to happen to him. In the final analysis, it is the designer who must keep himself from being imposed upon by an early declaration of his position.

The designer was referred to earlier as leader, not dictator. Just as it is important for the designer to realize that he cannot be dictatorial, so too must the client understand and respect the designer's role.

No doctor, no lawyer, no accountant would stand for the kind of interference that some clients attempt to impose on the designer. A businessman retaining a designer to plan and design his offices should do so only after thoroughly investigating the work of the designer. Having retained him he should have faith in his own judgment. The description of the camel as a throughbred race horse designed by a committee was not conceived out of thin air by a gag writer. It is the painful truth to many designers.

The budget that is submitted as part of the design presentation should be no surprise to the client if the original budget was a realistic one. Examined once more in conjunction with the design presentation, the budget may undergo some further revision downward—or upward. Some few clients approve a preliminary budget with the hope, unvoiced, that actual prices will prove to be less than the guesstimates. When actual costs prove to be as estimated the budget must then be pared to where it should have been pared originally. This unrealistic approach, on the part of a client, to a realistic budget should be discouraged by letting him know that he will be expected to pay for any additional design effort caused by his inability to face the budget problem at the time it was first discussed.

Other clients, delighted with the design presentation, decide to increase the budget and will augment the number of areas originally slated for design, as well as add to the list of new furniture and furnishings to be purchased. Whether added to or subtracted from, the budget will provide the purchasing program for the work to be done and the furniture and furnishings to be acquired. This will be fully discussed in Section III of this chapter.

Drawing 18

FURNITURE LEGEND

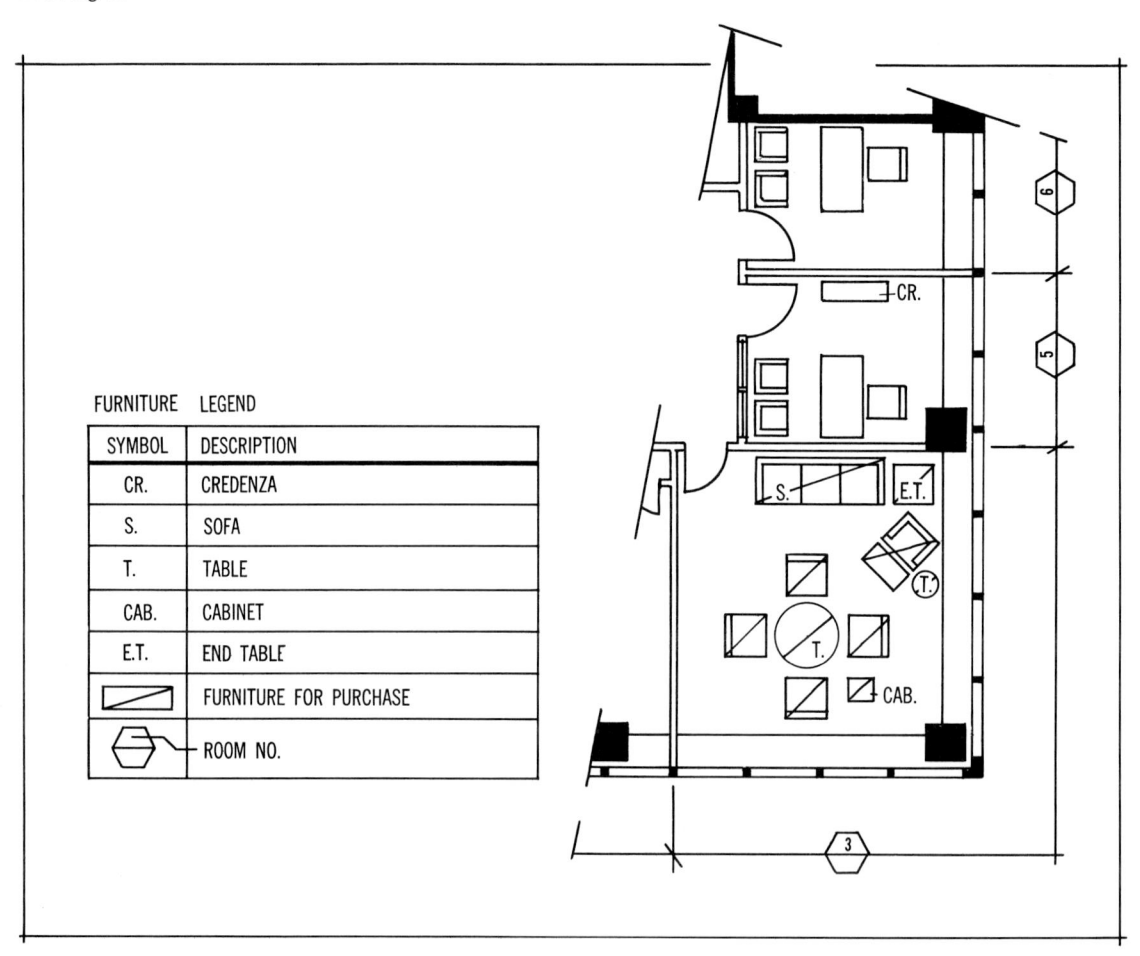

SYMBOL	DESCRIPTION
CR.	CREDENZA
S.	SOFA
T.	TABLE
CAB.	CABINET
E.T.	END TABLE
	FURNITURE FOR PURCHASE
	ROOM NO.

FURNITURE PLAN
ABC Corporation, Sales Division

This plan of part of the area rented by the ABC Corporation shows some of the furniture and equipment, existing and proposed. It is not a plan that will be part of the working drawing set, because it does not include the electrical and telephone outlets, nor does it indicate any required elevations or details. In order to clearly illustrate the furniture that must be on each plan, the rest of the information has been deleted. A furniture, telephone, and electrical plan is shown on Drawing 19.

Preparing 99
Working
Drawings

SECTION II   PREPARING WORKING DRAWINGS

With space study, design presentations, and budget approved, the next step will involve you in the preparation of the working drawings that will serve as the bidding and building documents. They will turn the dreams of your design into the three dimensions of reality.

Because this is not a textbook on architectural drafting, no attempt will be made to talk about any of the things that deal with drafting itself. Instead discussion will be confined to each of the drawings that must be part of the complete working-drawing set, and each drawing (numbers 18 through 22) in the text illustrates how the information it must contain should be indicated on the plan.

Checklist J—Working Drawings, at the end of this chapter, is a checklist of items that might be included on each of the plans. In addition to using the list to check required items, the personnel working on the drawings should be supplied with the list of items called for in the client's work letter. The work letter must be checked very carefully in order to make certain that the client gets everything to which he is entitled.

A good deal of information and work will be contributed by others before you will be able to call your working drawings complete. The information received from such people as the telephone company engineers will have to be shown on your plan. The drawings of structural and mechanical engineers should be coordinated by you into the working-drawing set. The areas in which each will make his contribution, the manner in which information will be supplied for this required engineering effort (air conditioning, electrical, and plumbing), and the way in which it will be coordinated with the balance of the plans will be described as each of the working drawings is discussed. Wherever it will be of help, you should be prepared to supply drawings to the engineers in **transparency** form.

You should, in fact, use transparencies as an aid and shortcut in your preparation of the working drawings. Each of the drawings required in the set of working drawings can be completed on transparencies made from the partition plan drawn after the space study has been approved. Drawing 18 shows a furniture plan prepared on such a partition plan.

The first plan to be prepared would be the furniture, telephone, and

Drawing 19

TELEPHONE AND ELECTRIC LEGEND

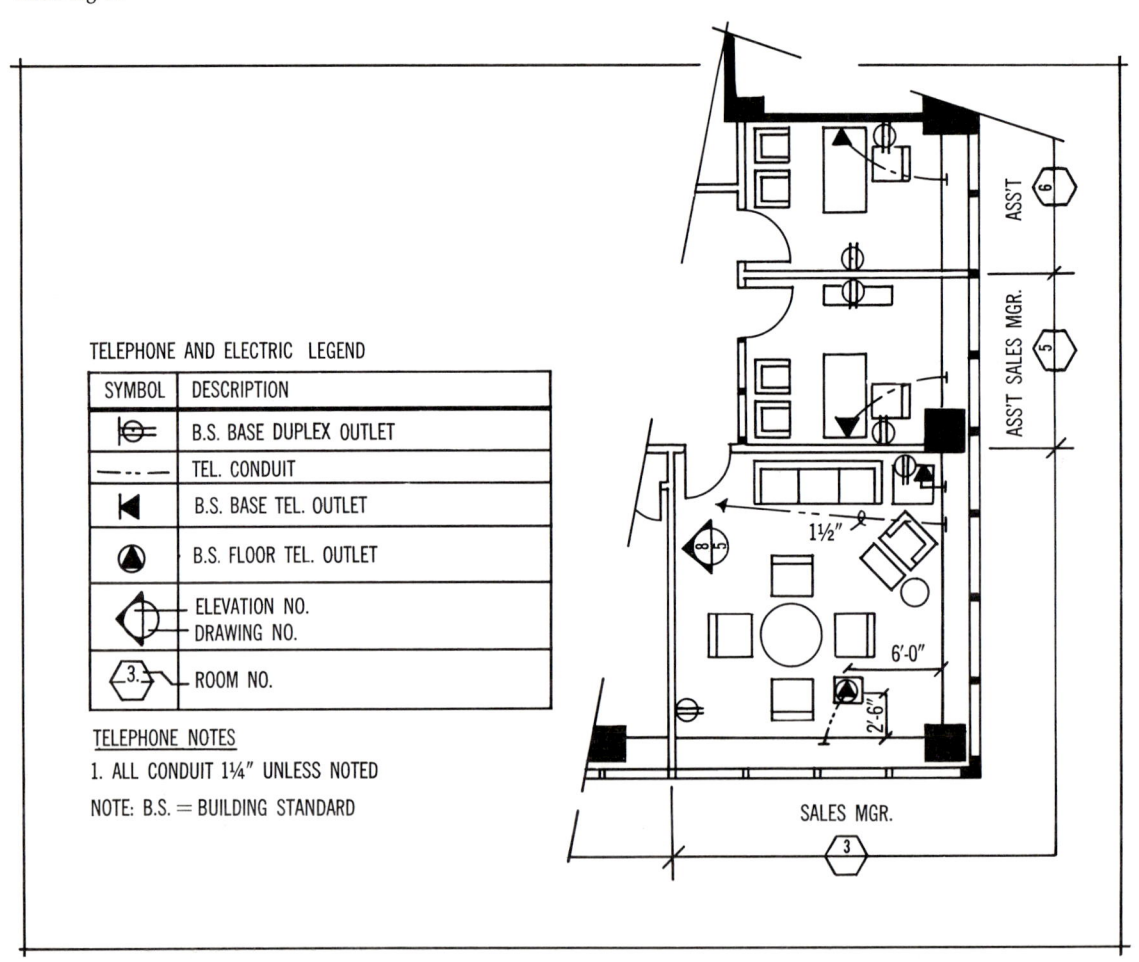

SYMBOL	DESCRIPTION
⊖	B.S. BASE DUPLEX OUTLET
— - —	TEL. CONDUIT
◀	B.S. BASE TEL. OUTLET
●	B.S. FLOOR TEL. OUTLET
◇	ELEVATION NO. / DRAWING NO.
⬢ 3	ROOM NO.

TELEPHONE NOTES
1. ALL CONDUIT 1¼" UNLESS NOTED
NOTE: B.S. = BUILDING STANDARD

WORKING DRAWING
Furniture, Telephone, and Electrical Plan — Partial
ABC Corporation, Sales Division

This and the balance of the drawings used to illustrate the plans that make up a complete set of working drawings is a partial plan showing only three offices—Rooms 3, 5, and 6. The legends are typical for each drawing and indicate the kind of information each should carry. The furniture legend shown on Drawing 18 would also appear on this plan.

electrical plan. Drawn on the transparency described above, it must delineate all the space-taking furniture and equipment inventoried as existing or proposed. This plan is prepared before the others because one of its many purposes is to validate the space study by proving that all the furniture actually fits within the spaces allotted to it. At times minor changes may have to be made to accommodate the equipment by making one room larger than anticipated and another smaller, but any required adjustments should be made before you begin work on any of the other plans that are part of the working-drawing set.

After the furniture has been located satisfactorily, the telephone and electrical information should be added to the plan. On it will be located, by dimension and symbol, all electrical and telephone outlets. By showing both of these on the furniture plan, you enjoy the obvious advantage of assuring the placement of electrical outlets where they are required and the placement of telephones where they will be used. A transparency of the plan should be supplied to the mechanical engineer for outlet circuiting.

The plan will show the location and size of the telephone-equipment room and the location of each outlet, each phone, jack, and switchboard. This should be prepared in cooperation with the client's telephone company business representative and the telephone company engineer, who will not only give you the information you need to include on the plan concerning the size and runs of required conduiting, but will also tell you whether there will be any excess floor-load problems in the equipment room.

The telephone-equipment room is not the only area where floor reinforcing may be needed. When you gather information concerning the building to which the client is moving, you should find out the floor-load capacity of the space. The furniture plan will show where a concentration of heavy equipment, such as data-processing machines, files, and storage, may dictate the need for strengthening the structure. If the building is not yet up or the finished floor not yet poured, it should be possible to add strength to the floor at that point of construction. Excess loads can be spread on finished floors with the use of steel plates or beams, or the loads can themselves be planned over existing structural members. In any event, load information indicated on the furniture plan should go to a structural engineer (either the building engineer or one retained to examine the

Drawing 20

CONSTRUCTION LEGEND

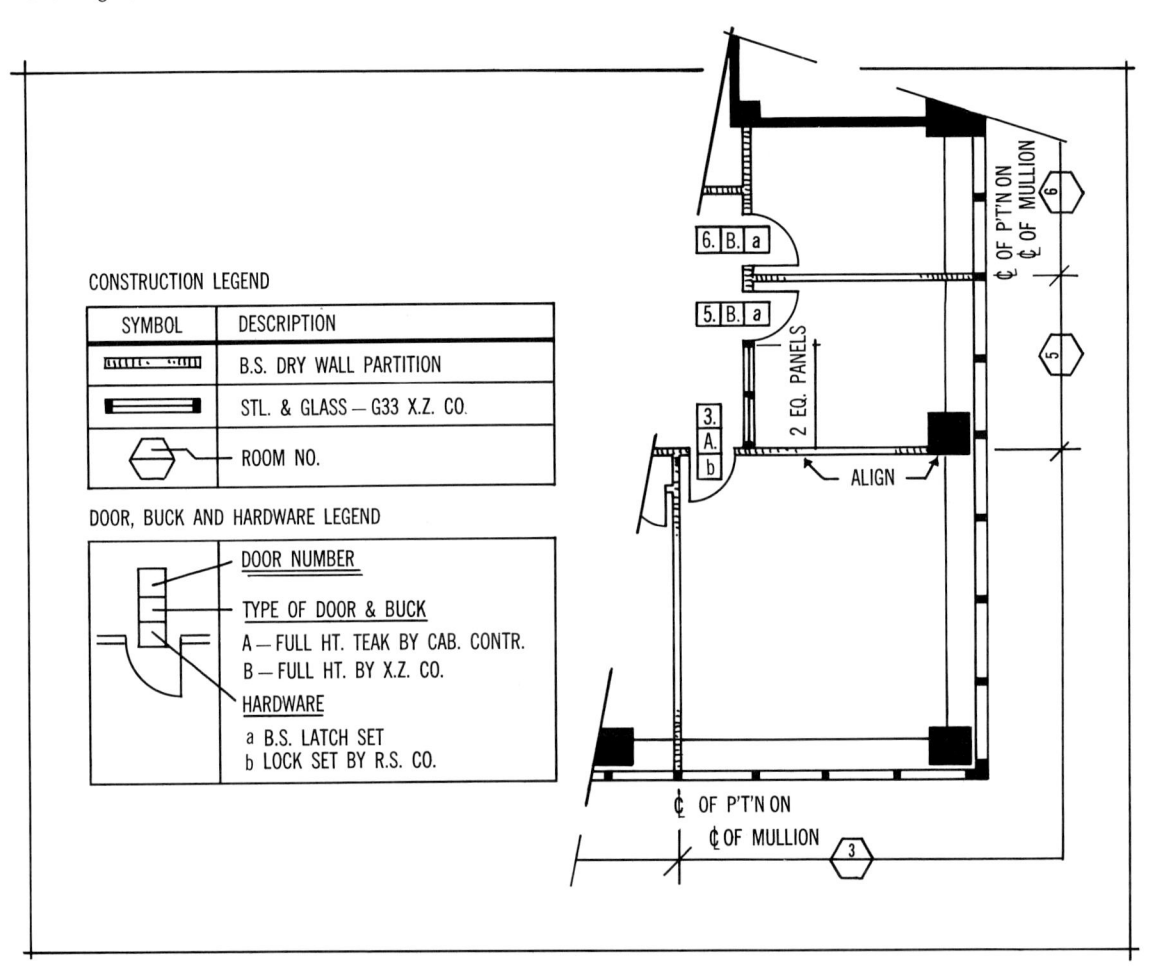

SYMBOL	DESCRIPTION
	B.S. DRY WALL PARTITION
	STL. & GLASS — G33 X.Z. CO.
⬡	ROOM NO.

DOOR, BUCK AND HARDWARE LEGEND

- DOOR NUMBER
- TYPE OF DOOR & BUCK
  A — FULL HT. TEAK BY CAB. CONTR.
  B — FULL HT. BY X.Z. CO.
- HARDWARE
  a B.S. LATCH SET
  b LOCK SET BY R.S. CO.

₵ OF P'T'N ON
₵ OF MULLION

2 EQ. PANELS

ALIGN

₵ OF P'T'N ON
₵ OF MULLION

WORKING DRAWING
Construction Plan — Partial
ABC Corporation, Sales Division

The construction plan shows partition and door information. If there is room on the sheet for construction details, they should be included. If not, they would be shown on one of the detail sheets. The general notes should indicate conformance with local codes and list any general requirements or instructions.

plans), so that he can prepare any drawings that may be needed or supply any structural advice that may be required.

Any areas that would require elevations and details for cabinetwork would be shown on the furniture plan, with symbol reference made to the particular sheet of cabinet details on which it appears.

The furniture plan should also be used to indicate which pieces of furniture are existing, which are to be purchased for use when the client moves into the space, and which will be purchased in the future. This will be of value as a check on the purchasing program and as the key plan for the actual move.

From this point on, the order in which you prepare the working drawings will depend on the dates agreed to in the lease or the pressures put on you by the schedules to be maintained. The total project can be hastened if you can deliver plan information to the structural and mechanical engineers as early as possible, so that their effort can be carried on concurrent with your completion of the balance of the working drawings.

The biggest jobs required of the structural engineer on most office planning projects will be those connected with floor reinforcing for load carrying or floor piercing for stairwells, dumbwaiters, private elevators, etc. Load information should go to the structural engineer on the furniture plan, while other structural information will go to him via the **construction plan.** The location of required floor piercing for stairwells between floors, dumbwaiters, private elevators, etc., will also be indicated on the construction plan and given to the engineer for any structural designing that may be required because of these installations.

The mechanical engineer is concerned with planning the heating and ventilating, the plumbing, and the electrical circuiting for the tenant space. It would therefore be best to supply the information he needs for his work as soon as possible. The **reflected ceiling plan** will give him needed data on air conditioning, and the plumbing information he needs will be shown on the construction plan. The engineer, given a copy of this plan showing the location and plumbing requirements for drinking fountains, sinks, private toilets, kitchens, darkrooms, etc., will prepare the plumbing drawings needed for their installation. These drawings will then be coordinated with the other working drawings.

The construction plan will be prepared, like the rest of the drawings, on a partition-plan transparency. On it will be located, by dimension and

Drawing 21

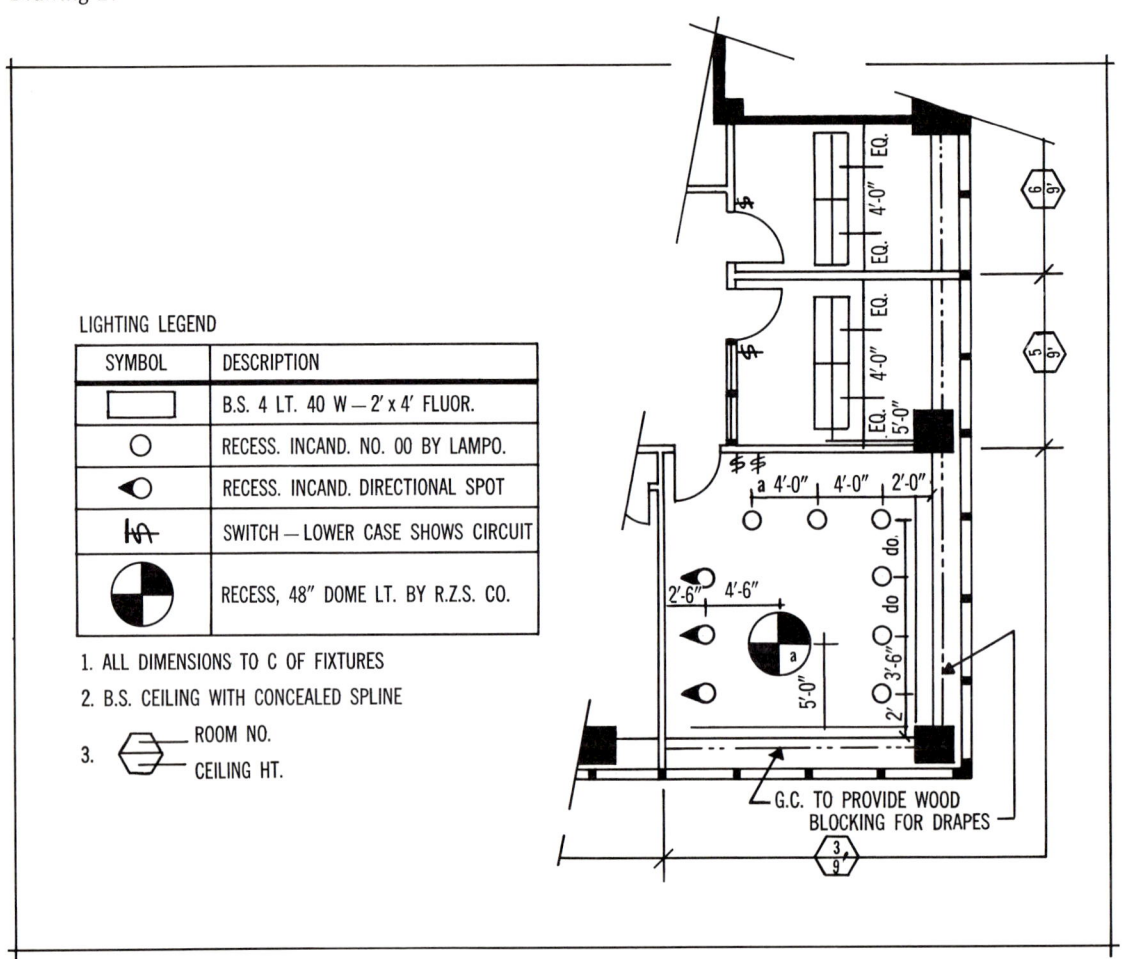

LIGHTING LEGEND

SYMBOL	DESCRIPTION
▭	B.S. 4 LT. 40 W — 2' x 4' FLUOR.
○	RECESS. INCAND. NO. 00 BY LAMPO.
◐	RECESS. INCAND. DIRECTIONAL SPOT
⌐	SWITCH — LOWER CASE SHOWS CIRCUIT
◓	RECESS, 48" DOME LT. BY R.Z.S. CO.

1. ALL DIMENSIONS TO C OF FIXTURES
2. B.S. CEILING WITH CONCEALED SPLINE
3. ⬡ — ROOM NO. / CEILING HT.

WORKING DRAWING
Reflected Ceiling Plan — Partial
ABC Corporation, Sales Division

This is the plan that indicates all the ceiling lights, their switches and all other elements, except air conditioning, that are part of the ceiling system.
A transparency of it should be sent to the mechanical engineer for his work in preparing schematic air-conditioning drawings and light circuiting. This plan should also include unusual heat loads from equipment or any large concentration of people. Any required details for wood blocking would be shown on this sheet or on one of the detail sheets.

symbol, all of the types of partitions and doors that are to be used in the space. Complete specifications for the doors will be shown in detail on the door, buck, and hardware schedule. This schedule is described in Checklist J, at the end of this chapter.

This plan will also contain whatever special details of construction are required. These would not include **cabinet details,** which will be shown on separate detail drawings described later. The most common of the details that would appear on the construction plan would be those of any special door bucks, wall openings for pass-through windows, or any other details needed to describe odd or unusual construction elements.

The reflected ceiling plan shows all lighting fixtures, located by dimensions and specified by symbol. It will also show the location of all switches, dimmer controls, etc. The desired ceiling heights of each room should be indicated on this plan, along with any construction or design details that may have to be part of the ceiling or used in the ceiling breaks at the point where ceiling heights change. Details of wood blocking for sliding-door mechanisms or anything else that is to be ceiling hung should be shown on this plan.

The plan should also indicate which rooms, such as conference rooms and classrooms, will have more than normal people occupancy and which rooms will contain heat-producing equipment for which allowance must be made by the air-conditioning engineers. The plan should also show specific requirements that may exist for any special air conditioning, such as thermostatic controls, reheat coils, and humidity controls.

The completed reflected ceiling plan should then be given to the mechanical engineer in transparency form. It is from this plan that he will develop his schematic duct plan for his engineering drawings. On it he will also indicate the electric circuiting necessary for switches and the fixtures they control.

The last of the basic set of working drawings is the **paint and flooring plan.** This plan should show the paint and wall covering to be installed on all wall surfaces and the materials to be installed on the floors. It will also carry information concerning the installation of draperies and blinds.

The working drawings are augmented by the **elevations** and **details** of construction and cabinetwork that is to be installed on the job. These detail drawings should include whatever notes are needed to provide for the coordination of cabinetwork with other trades. The details should be keyed to the numbers and symbols used on the furniture plan.

Drawing 22

PAINT AND WALL COVERING LEGEND

NO.	MAT'R'L	M'F'R	NO.	COLOR	REMARKS
1.	TEAK			OIL FIN.	BY CAB. CONTR.
2.	VINYL	JAY	233	WHITE	
3.	VINYL	JAY	63	BEIGE	
4.	CORK	MAR			CONTEMPO
5.	PAINT	P & L	256	WHITE	SEMIGLOSS

WALL COVERING LEGEND

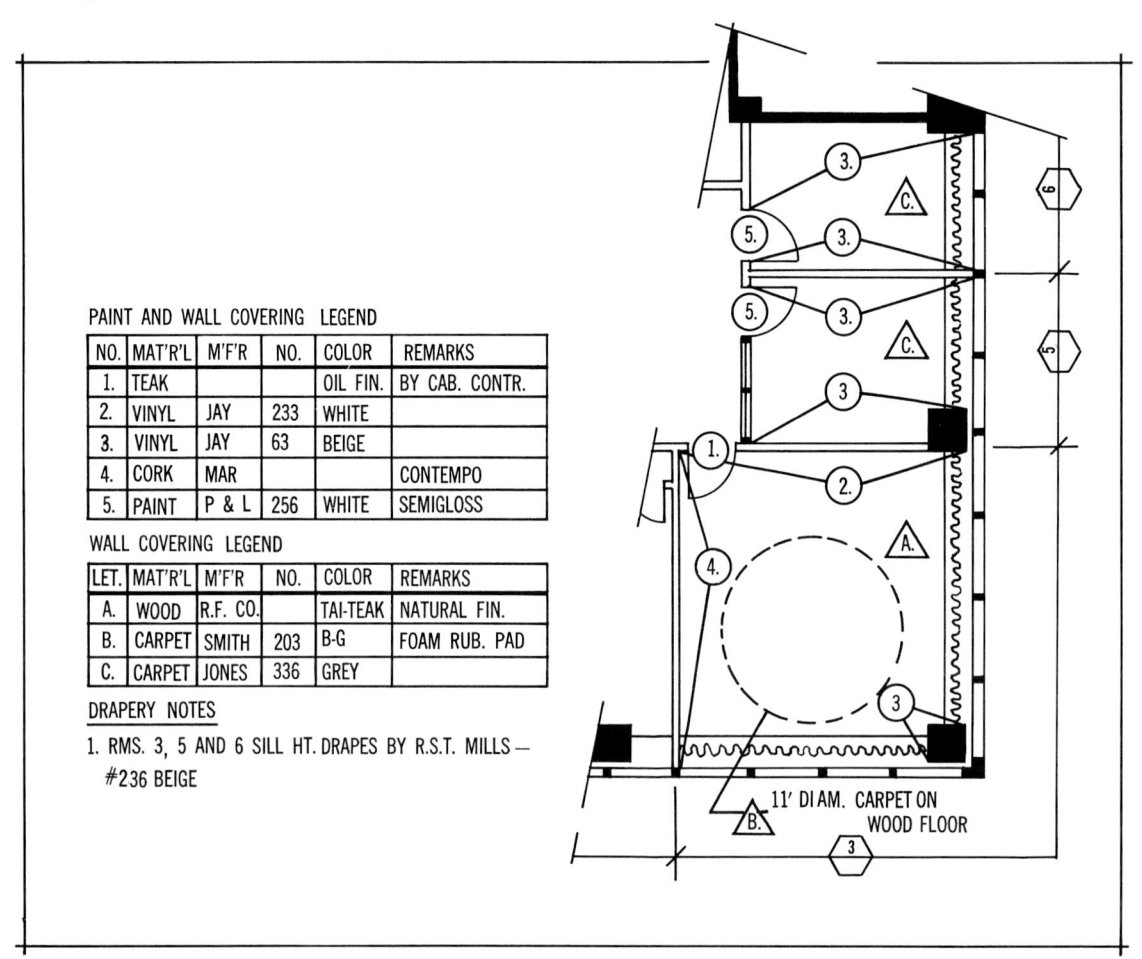

LET.	MAT'R'L	M'F'R	NO.	COLOR	REMARKS
A.	WOOD	R.F. CO.		TAI-TEAK	NATURAL FIN.
B.	CARPET	SMITH	203	B-G	FOAM RUB. PAD
C.	CARPET	JONES	336	GREY	

DRAPERY NOTES

1. RMS. 3, 5 AND 6 SILL HT. DRAPES BY R.S.T. MILLS — #236 BEIGE

11' DIAM. CARPET ON WOOD FLOOR

WORKING DRAWING
Paint and Flooring Plan — Partial
ABC Corporation, Sales Division

All wall covering, flooring, bases, saddles, and drapery specifications are shown on this plan. The wall covering includes paint, vinyl, mirror, and any other finish that will be used on the wall. Walls requiring work on the part of the cabinet contractor will be indicated on this plan and on the furniture plan. Required elevations and details will be illustrated on the detail sheets.

Although each plan in the set of working drawings illustrates information peculiar to it, the drawings are completely interrelated. Rarely can a change be made on one without causing changes on others. You must make certain through careful plan checking that any such possible chain reaction is fully recorded on all plans. A change in position of an electrical outlet may require a position change in a piece of furniture, which might, in turn, force a change in a ceiling light fixture and a telephone outlet. To change one plan without checking its effect on the other plans could be slightly catastrophic if construction is completed before the problems are caught.

A client's expressed need for flexibility in his overall layout is another thing that can affect all the plans. If true flexibility is desired, it will not usually be accomplished merely by specifying movable partitions on the construction plan. Flexibility can be accomplished only if you anticipate all the items that will be related to the move of a partition and provide for them in advance. This could include lights, switches, electrical and telephone outlets, ceilings, flooring, and air conditioning.

SECTION III   PREPARING A PURCHASING PROGRAM

Purchasing, as it is described here, is separate from the bidding and letting of contracts for building-trade work. The program is centered around furniture, equipment, carpets, drapes, ashtrays, wastebaskets, pictures, and all the other things that must be ordered (or noted for later ordering) and delivered as scheduled in coordination with the client's move-in date.

The list of things to be purchased will be made up first from the inventory and then from the design presentation, with the budget used as a checklist to make certain that everything has been included. Some clients prefer to do all the purchasing through their own facilities. In that case, the purchase list with all the supporting information shown on the **authorization form** would be given to the client. Whether you do the ordering for the client or the client does his own, it is up to you to check out the availability of all the items that are to be purchased, making certain that all fabrics are or will be in stock, all furniture available in reasonable time

Drawing 23

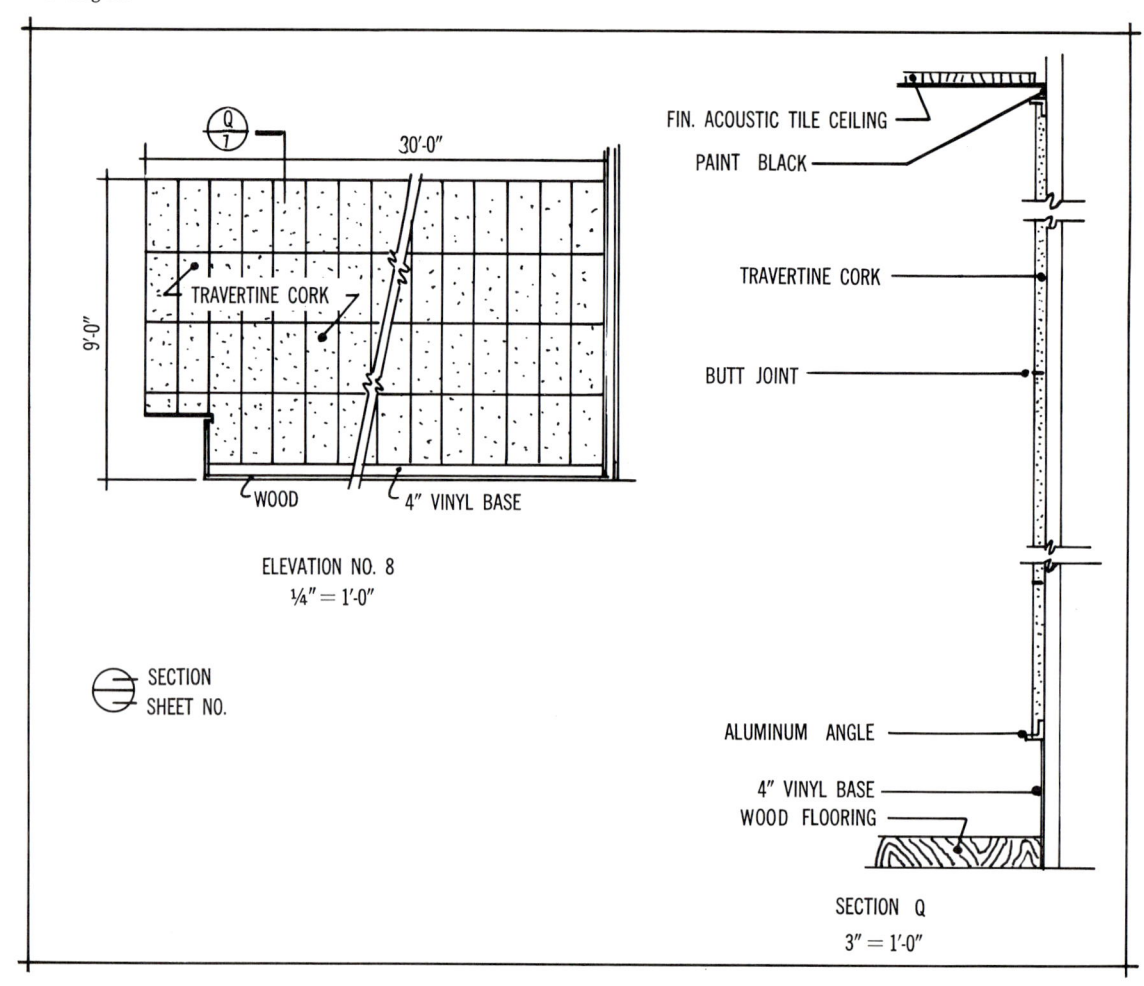

WORKING DRAWINGS
Elevations and Details — Partial
ABC Corporation, Sales Division

The illustration shows the wall of Room 3 that was indicated for detailing on Drawing 19. The section is of the same wall. The notes are instructions to the cabinet contractor. They can be added to as need dictates.

all carpets still being produced, etc. It is also important to make certain that no price changes have taken place since last you inquired and that none are contemplated prior to your actual ordering.

Much of what you will order will take many months to obtain, and it would be wise to get your orders out to the manufacturers as soon as possible after you have client approval. Ideally the orders should be sent out while the working drawings are in preparation. Once the design presentation and its accompanying budget have been approved, the authorization forms, spelling out exactly what is to be purchased and its cost, should be signed by the client, authorizing you thereby to purchase the furniture for him.

The form should describe each item to be purchased, its source and catalog number, the unit price, and the extension of that price. Each line should have a space for client initaling, so that each item can be individually approved. The form should also indicate that prices are subject to delivery charges, and should show any pertinent sales or excise taxes. For the purpose of double-checking the fact that authorized items have been purchased, space should be provided on each line for the inclusion of a **purchase order** number to be filled in when the order is issued.

Every designer at one time or another ends up with a few extra pieces of furniture in his own office because he failed to get the client's signed authorization prior to ordering furniture. There really is no more bitter way to learn the importance of the authorization form.

When you make out the form (and from it the purchase order), you should check and recheck manufacturers' numbers, colors, finishes, descriptions, etc., to ensure that the correct item in the correct color, with the correct finish, is being ordered. The inadvertent transposition of numbers or the misreading of a color can cause all kinds of unnecessary problems. Some designers insist that the fabric supplier enclose swatches with his acknowledgment of the order.

A copy of the authorization form should be left with the client as his check on his own expenditure, as a check on the purchase order, and as a check on the eventual invoice for the items authorized. The purchase order, numbered, is most conveniently kept in multicarbon form. One copy goes to the client for his records, one to the supplier, and one is for your own accounting record. A fourth copy should go to the **project**

director, and a fifth is kept by the **expediter.** The purchase order itself, in addition to describing the merchandise to be ordered, its quantity, and its amount, should carry all shipping instructions, billing instructions, and sample instructions. The logistics of getting all the furniture delivered when it is supposed to be delivered is the expediter's job. He is responsible for seeing that furniture, fabrics, ashtrays, water coolers, etc., all arrive when they are supposed to. He is also responsible for making certain that the fabric gets to the upholsterer in time to get the chair to the client in time for him to sit in it when he moves into his new offices.

The record keeping necessary to assure proper on-time delivery is a routine task of regularly checking sources of supply to make certain that all is being done. A good expediter will set up a system of advance checks, so that there will be as few last-minute unpleasant surprises as possible. The delivery of a chair will be checked not on the day delivery is expected, but several times, and at varying intervals, prior to that date.

CHECKLIST I   DESIGN PRESENTATION

Much of the checklist material covered earlier will be checked again to make certain that everything already requested has been included in the presentation. The minutes taken when you reviewed the list of design and construction requirements, the revised preliminary budget, and the work letter of the lease will have to be checked off to make certain that each item has been made part of the presentation.

Before preparing the presentation you should, with the approved space study in front of you, compile a list of the material that will be needed to complete the presentation. This list will contain a description of:

1. Each individual room or area requiring furniture layout.

2. Each individual room or area requiring perspective renderings in color.

3. Each individual room or area requiring a perspective rendering or renderings in black-and-white.

4. Any sketches required.

5. Elevation required.

6. Any detailed drawings required.

Checklist I   111
Design
Presentation

7. Each design board required.

8. Any required plans to illustrate wall and floor finishes and colors.

Each design board must be checked to make certain that it contains (when applicable):

1. Samples of wall colors and finishes.
2. Sample of flooring.
3. Photographs of all furniture.
4. Samples of wood finishes for both furniture and cabinetwork.
5. Samples of metal finishes and laminates for furniture and cabinetwork.
6. Samples of fabric for furniture.
7. Samples of fabrics for drapes.
8. Photographs and samples (where possible) of accessories.
9. Photographs or samples of any other items that are part of the design of the room or area, including signs and wall decorations.

Each item on each design board must be clearly labeled and identified with the plan or rendering that it helps clarify. In fact each board or drawing or plan that is part of the presentation must be titled, so that it can be understood by the client and his people when you are not present to discuss it with them. Often the client will take the drawings and design boards to his office to show it to others who were not present at the original presentation.

If you follow the idea of using one standard form of identification for people and areas on all documents, starting with the first requirements taken, you should have little trouble identifying titles and numbers in your presentation. And, when the time comes, you should even be able to use these for the instructions that will be given to the company hired to do the actual furniture moving for the client.

CHECKLIST J   WORKING DRAWINGS

This checklist is arranged according to the requirements of each plan in the set of working drawings, and includes a section on general notes. Some designers will include notes, legends, schedules, etc., on each of the drawings pertinent to the particular notes. Others prefer to keep the drawings separate from the notes, with the notes made part of a specifications document. No matter what the form, the listed items should help to decide what should or should not be included in the set of working drawings.

The title box that will be standard on all of your drawings should be designed to allow for easy job-number and drawing identification. Original dates should be clearly marked, as should dates of each revision.

It is important to try to adhere to the identifying numbers used at the outset when you first listed organizational requirements. The room numbers used in the space study (and which came originally from the listed requirements) should be maintained on all plans and details. The doors, bucks, and hardware will be identified by these numbers, as will **shop drawings** and details, and they will be used for the identification of furniture to be moved or purchased.

1. **General Notes**

    These are usually made a part of the construction plan and are concerned primarily with information indicating that the drawings were done in conformity with local building and fire regulations. Since most locations require that plans be filed with, and jobs eventually be inspected by, the various responsible local agencies, all work must conform to the local **building codes.**

    The applicable sections and paragraphs of the local codes are referred to in describing the installation of such things as hung ceilings, corridor partitions, fireproof wood, fire-resistive doors, and directional signs. Floor occupancy and any other code-required information should be made part of these general notes.

    The notes should also indicate, if pertinent, that all dimensions should be checked and verified in the field by the contractors and subcontractors, before any prefabrications or installations are made.

2. **Furniture, Telephone, and Electrical Plan**

    Furniture legend carries:
    (a) Symbol and description of all existing furniture and equipment.
    (b) Symbol and description of all furniture and equipment to be purchased.
    (c) Symbol and description of all furniture and equipment to be purchased in the future.

    Telephone legend carries:
    (a) Symbols and descriptions of the telephone instruments and equipment.

(b) Symbols and description of telephone conduits.
(c) Notes concerning any other requirements for telephone installation.
Electrical legend carries:
(a) Symbols and description of electrical outlets.
(b) Symbols and description of other electrical installation (other than ceiling installations), such as door buzzers, push buttons, paging systems, and in-use lights.

3. **Construction Plan**
   Construction legend carries:
   (a) Symbol and description of all types of partitions to be used, including building-standard partition.
   (b) Location and description of drinking fountains and any other plumbing equipment needed.
   (c) Location and description of any carpentry required as basic construction, such as wood shelves and chrome poles in clothes closets, and wood grounds.
   (d) Sound baffling, where required, above partitions from hung ceiling to slab of floor above.
   Door, buck, and hardware legend carries:
   (a) The type of door and buck by identifying number, letter, and description.
   (b) The type of hardware to be used, identified by letter and description.
   (c) A general note concerning the undercutting of doors to accommodate carpeting.

4. **Reflected Ceiling Plan**
   Lighting legend carries:
   (a) Symbol and description of all lighting fixtures, including building-standard fixtures.
   (b) Symbols and description of all switches and dimmers.
   (c) Symbols and description of all other ceiling-installed electrical devices, such as loudspeakers, buzzers, paging systems, and microphones.
   Notes carry:
   (a) Information concerning dimensions.
   (b) Information concerning systems for hung ceiling.
   (c) Information concerning blocking for shelving, doors, walls, blinds, drapes, etc.

5. **Paint and Flooring Plan**
   Paint and wall-covering legend carries:
   (a) Identification by key number of the material, manufacturer, or supplier, manufacturer's number (if any), and color of all finishing material or paint to be used on the walls.

(b) Specific instructions required for installation of any floor or wall material.

Floor-covering legend carries:

Information as above, except that the identification would be by letter, rather than number, in order to avoid confusion.

Paint and wall-covering notes carry:

Instructions concerning surfaces other than those covered in the legend, such as:
- (a) door bucks
- (b) ceiling diffusers and registers
- (c) outlet covers
- (d) radiators
- (e) metal parts

Also the notes will carry instructions for submission of samples and the checking of colors.

Floor-covering notes carry:

Instructions concerning bases, reducing strips, saddles, floor patching, underlaying, protection of surfaces prior to move, etc.

Drapery notes carry:

General instructions covering drawing of drapes, height of drapes, and any required methods of installation.

6. **Elevations and Details**

This page (or pages) of drawings would show the elevations indicated on the furniture plan and all of the details and sections necessary to explain what is wanted and how it is to be constructed. The furniture plan must be checked to make certain that all elevations have been included.

The notes to the cabinet contractor would include instructions for compliance with local codes for submitting wood samples and finishes for the preparation of wood surfaces, the coordination with other trades such as the electrical contractor, and for submitting shop drawings for designer approval.

space, will be the coordinating effort that gives shape to all that has been done before.

It is a time of awarding bids, of checking shop drawings, and of overseeing the building. It is a time of watching walls go up, lights go in, and carpeting go down. It is a time of supplying, delivering, and installing.

And, end of all, it is the time when the doors open wide on the offices that you have planned and designed. It is the time when your client moves in to give reality to all the effort that has gone before. ∎

SECTION I   COORDINATING THE BIDDING

Obtaining bids on the work to be done is the first of many coordinating phases of the job that follow the completion of working drawings. The list of contractors and suppliers invited to bid usually includes companies that the designer knows to be reliable and whose work and prices have always been satisfactory, plus any contractors or suppliers from whom the client wants the designer to get bids. In new multiple-occupancy buildings, the general contractor hired by the owner to do both the tenant work and the basic building work is called the **contractor of record.** If there is a contractor of record doing work for the landlord, it will not be possible for you to get competitive bids on the general contracting work. But even when there is a contractor of record, bids must be obtained from those trades that are not part of the general contractor's effort, such as carpeting, cabinetwork, and special-equipment installations.

When the working drawings have been completed, **instructions to bidders** will be prepared and the drawings, specifications, and instructions sent to the invited bidders. The instructions may contain due dates of bids, completion dates for the work, any special coordination instructions, insurance requirements, trade-union requirements, the logistics of area completion if the job is in existing space, and any number of other things that may affect the bidding and the completion of the job. The instructions will spell out the bidders' responsibility for abiding by local building rules and regulations and for obtaining and paying for permits and filing fees. It will also list any special sources or subcontractors that are to be asked to submit bids to the general contractor. In order to have the bidding conform to the budget and make it easier to check the prices against that budget, the instructions to bidders should also include a proposal form to be filled out by the bidders. This form should indicate a subdivision of bidding into the major trades and categories shown on the budget form.

If a particular job involves a fairly large expenditure of money, **sealed bids,** opened in the presence of the client, may be a sensible way of assuring the contractors that all bidders have an equal opportunity to be awarded the job. Whether this procedure is followed on smaller jobs should be the client's decision.

The manner in which the costs for extra work are handled when the basic work is being done by the landlord has been discussed on page 77.

Coordinating the Bidding

When the bids or landlord's costs come in, they should undergo careful checking against the budget estimates, so that any unusual discrepancies can be discovered.

If, as has happened, one cabinetmaker's bid is far higher than the budgeted amount (and therefore out of line with all other bidders), you may discover that the cabinet man is figuring on an unnecessarily complicated method of construction. This can then be corrected so as to bring his price into line competitively.

In one case a carpet bid was ridiculously low. Close examination proved that several rooms had been inadvertently left out of the bid. Had the designer allowed the client to accept the contract as it stood, everybody would have felt very happy about saving money—but not for long. A later unexpected extra charge would have been very unpleasant for the designer, the supplier, and the client.

Further coordination of the effort contributed by others is accomplished by checking the engineering drawings and the cabinet contractor's shop drawings.

The engineering drawings are checked to make certain that the air-conditioning installation provides for all the special things that have been requested, such as conference-room exhausts and after-hours equipment. You must also be certain that it allows for the ceiling heights needed and that all diffusers, grilles, anemostats, thermostats, etc., are placed in such a way as to conform with the overall design desire. Your primary concern is with the visual aspects of any part of the mechanical engineering, and you must be prepared to consult with the engineer in order to arrive at solutions that will satisfy both design and function.

Sometimes the engineering drawing will make you and the client aware of problems that were not apparent. One client moving from an old to a new building was forced to provide inside offices for two of his most important private secretaries. These were girls who had had window offices and who were always opening and closing windows when they were too hot or too cold. The client was not concerned about the reaction to no windows but became concerned when the engineering drawings pointed out that the girls, in their new offices, would be unable to control the temperature of their areas. The air-conditioning system would not allow for individual control. Undaunted (but a little ashamed of the subterfuge), management, engineer, and designer contrived to install thermostats in each of the girls' offices. When the girls were uncomfortable, they regulated the thermostats, unaware of the fact that the thermostats do not work and have never been attached to anything except the wall. They are happy and the client is happy.

Cabinet-contractor shop drawings should be examined not only to allow the designer the opportunity to check on the work the contractor is doing, but also to allow him to make changes in details, dimensions, and design to accommodate any field conditions that may have arisen.

You should be prepared to check any shop or engineering drawings that are extensions of your designs or that would affect your design. At times, contractors or suppliers will ask the designer to check door schedules or hardware schedules or similar lists of materials to be supplied. Some designers do this checking, but others refuse on the ground that the schedules are merely copies of the designer's original schedule translated to the supplier's information form. They reason, therefore, that it is not the designer's job to check on the accuracy of the supplier's translation.

After all the bids are in, checked, and discussed with the client, awards should be made (the manner in which they are made is described below), and schedules set up for the start of the job.

The manner in which bids are awarded can vary according to client desires. Most clients are satisfied to sign the contractor or supplier proposals, but some prefer to issue their own purchase orders. The designer should handle the transmittal of bid acceptance, no matter what its form, so that the contractor or supplier is aware of the designer's role as client's agent in the supervision of his efforts. Any other system can only weaken designer authority and make you less effective as agent for the client. The instructions given to the contractor or supplier to whom the bid has been awarded include the fact that all invoices and statements should be addressed to the client, in care of the designer. All payments should then be made only after the designer has passed the bills on to the client and approved them for payment, either in whole or in part, depending upon his agreement or disagreement with the amount and quality of the work completed.

SECTION II COORDINATING THE BUILDING

It is very easy to predict that from the start of construction in the client's space until its completion something unforeseen will happen every day! The daily problems, large or small, dictate the necessity for some daily supervision. How each designer manages this depends on the way in which he organizes his effort and the size of his staff.

Each **supervisor** should keep a **progress chart** that will serve as a report to personnel in his own office and to the client, if the client wishes to be kept abreast of construction and installation at periodic intervals. The chart, devised primarily as an aid to the supervisor, will be particularly valuable to him when he is supervising many jobs at the same time. It should be designed to show at a glance whether the job is progressing according to the predetermined schedule.

If it is not, it should clearly pinpoint the inefficiencies of the contractor's effort. The chart can list trades in as detailed a fashion as each individual project may require. For example, air conditioning can be so listed or it can be subdivided into duct work, air-handling equipment, grilles, anemostats, enclosures, etc.

Another important part of the supervisor's effort is his involvement in the sequential preparation of areas as they are needed to accommodate other trades. A case in point is the room required to house the client's telephone equipment. The installation of this equipment can take many, many weeks and even months. The actual length of time should be determined at the outset of the job, so that the equipment room can be made ready early enough (and in advance of the rest of the space if necessary) to allow for the timely completion of the telephone work.

Similar advance completion of areas may be necessary to allow for installation in screening room, data-processing areas, darkrooms, laboratories, etc. The exact lead time required for each must be worked into the logistics of space preparation.

Each client will have his own way of coping with this tension-provoking phase of the work. Some never go near the job until they are ready to move in. Others visit the site only occasionally, and still others are at the job for many more hours than the designer. The first method is the most intelligent, but there seems to be no effective cure for the latter. If it can't be cured an attempt should be made to at least curb some of its evils. Clients should be warned not to give instructions to any workmen. Only the designer's supervisor should be empowered to order changes or additions and then only after he obtains costs for the work to be done and written authorization from the client for this expenditure. Only in this way can you protect the client by controlling the progress of the job and the costs of it. Contractors and suppliers should certainly be ordered not to accept on-the-job changes unless they are confirmed by written authorization from the client passed on to them by the designer. Above all they should accept no signed authorizations that have no price attached. Too often pleasant jobs have turned unpleasant when, after the work was done, clients received bills which they believed to be excessive. Whether or not they were excessive is then past rational discussion; the work should not have been done without the client's knowledge and agreement to the cost. Many designers have their supervisory personnel carry job authorization forms with them at all times, so that on-the-job requests can be written up, priced, and authorized as rapidly as possible. Copies of the form should go to the client, the contractor, and the designer's **accounting department,** project director, and **technical drafting department,** so that the original drawings can be amended to reflect the changes to be made.

It is vital that both the accounting department and technical drafting be kept up to date on any field changes or revisions. Lack of communication during the building stage can cause all sorts of unfortunate and unnecessary problems in later changes, as well as in billing for the work done.

The single change of an electrical-outlet location may bring about a chain reaction that could include changes in the location of furniture, cabinetwork, telephone outlets, and ceiling lighting. Unless the technical draftsman has been told of the first change, the rest of the changes may not be made early enough to avoid costly and annoying field changes after the original installation has been made. If the accounting department is not informed of the changes, you will not be doing an adequate job of cost control for the client, and you may not be paid for authorized, chargeable change-effort.

The period of building and the period during and after the move are periods of difficulty for most clients. Since you as the planner and designer have been retained to see the client through these periods, it is incumbent upon you to do just that, and to do it with tact and understanding. Clients, walking through the space they will soon be occupying, sometimes become aware of things that were not apparent to them from their inexpert examination of plans. The client may suddenly realize that he needs another electrical outlet in the mail room or that it would be better to have his worktable behind him instead of next to him. These logical changes, additions, or deletions should be arranged expeditiously.

The service you render is just that, and you should be willing and eager to take on the details and worries and problems of a move for the client who has retained you to do so. The day-to-day problems of building that are met by the supervisor, the installation mistakes that are caught and rectified, and the schedules that can be and are maintained only because you are willing to expend unanticipated time to see that they are, are never reported to the client if you are truly doing your job of keeping him free of worry.

Field supervision is mainly a coordination of effort with the general contractor, the trades under him, and any other contracting or supplying effort. A good supervisor will arrange to visit a job at the same time each day, in order to meet job foremen for the various trades involved. In this way the key people representing client and contractors can meet the daily contingencies of the job. A supervisor, thoroughly familiar with the plans, the design, and the philosophy behind the job, should be empowered to make construction decisions that will not affect outward appearance. However, when he is faced with possible design decisions, he should consult with both the project director and the **project designer** before presenting any ideas to the client or permitting any changes to be made.

While the new space is being built, the client should make preparations in his existing offices for the move into his new quarters. Some of the activities in preparing to move are peculiarly client ones, and others involve your efforts to expedite the move. A complete move-in checklist is appended to this chapter as **Checklist K.** It covers both client and designer responsibilities, including a description of the "pre-move" activity on the part of the actual movers.

The final phase of the supervisory effort centers around the delivery and installation of purchased items that should be in before the client's move is complete. The purchasing should all have been done some time ago and specific delivery dates set up at that time. The schedule of delivery and installation can be simple to work out or, in the case of a client taking a large amount of space, it can be an exercise in logistics: carpeting goes down, drapes go up, furniture goes in, and all in logical sequence. The expediter will have checked and double-checked to make sure that everything will be ready to be delivered on the proper day and at the proper time.

It will take involvement in only one or two jobs for you to learn that, no matter how sincere the promises seem to be, on the day delivery is to be made the trucks break down! All experienced designers are aware of the fact that there are more broken-down trucks than there are trucks. And it is this nondelivery of any item that goes to help make up the finished product that makes this phase the most exasperating and frustrating part of the total job effort. A broken promise, when the promise didn't have to be made in the first place, comes as close to being inexcusable as anything could be. As the designer to whom such promises will be often made and often broken, you should learn not to make promises to your client unless you are sure they can be kept.

Occasionally, despite exasperations, frustrations, and anxieties, amusing things can happen at delivery time.

One client, who was moving enough of his old furniture into his new quarters to allow him to operate, had to have new conference-room furniture—table and chairs—delivered by 10 a.m. on the Monday morning after his weekend move. Although the client had tried to avoid it, a very important meeting had to be scheduled for that Monday. For weeks the designer had been checking with the supplier of the conference-room furniture, and for weeks he had been promised on-time delivery from their out-of-town plant. On Friday and Saturday everything else had been delivered and installed. On Monday designer staff men were waiting at the client's office for the conference-room furniture to arrive. At 9:15 the supplier called the designer's office to inform him that, through an error in shipping instructions at the plant, it would be another three days before the table and chairs would arrive. Ten people in the design office had apoplexy, the expediter came close to having a heart attack, and Mr. Bell would have regretted having invented the telephone if he could have heard the language and the loud voices his phone carried that morning. While all this was going on, the client called to tell the designer how delighted he was with the conference-room furniture that had just arrived. No one ever did discover what really had happened!

Prior to the actual move, it would be well to advise the client to go through an orientation session with his personnel. This can be accomplished in many ways, and can include a tour of the new space or the distribution of personalized plans to each employee with verbal or written description of the whys and wherefores of the planning, of the new furniture, and of the new equipment.

One particularly good method is to have the designer explain the features of the new space and the reasons behind much of the planning and design. Adroitly handled, this can serve as a wonderful public relations tool. It will help to give the employees the pride they should have in their new offices and give them pride, too, in their advance participation in the preparation for the move. It will give each employee an understanding of what has been done and make possible an orderly start of routine business the day after the move.

SECTION III COORDINATING THE MOVING

The smooth execution of an office move depends upon the clear delineation of the things to be done and the assignment of responsibility for getting them done. Most of the work will have to be done by the client's people and the mover, with an assist from the space planner. The client should establish a **moving committee** consisting of people thoroughly familiar with the company's personnel and its operation. Each member of the committee will have many things to take care of, and each should be given the power to make whatever decisions are necessary to keep the move going.

The size of the committee will depend upon the size of the company. Its effort will be augmented by the mover and his people, with the space planner helping where he can. A meeting of all three should be arranged as early as possible, in order to make certain that all phases of the move are known and their accomplishment planned.

If all of the furniture and files and typewriters and wastebaskets that are to be moved have been properly labeled, the move itself is a rather simple, although tiring, affair. The tensions build as the cartons pile up in the new offices and the client is faced with the problem of what to do first. Anyone who has ever moved a home, an apartment, or an office knows the panic and frustration of facing a task that has no obvious beginning and no foreseeable end. Fortunately, it is usually only momentary panic that disappears once the physical effort of filing, storing, and putting things in desk drawers begins.

The real headaches are something else again. They vary from problems of dissatisfaction with color, a missing switch plate, or files that do not fit in the space provided for them. Most are blown up out of proportion to their true importance by the excitement and turmoil of the move itself. The designer must be ready to make fast decisions. He must placate the client and postpone action on many things until time can either give validity to the desired changes or make them unnecessary. He must also quickly decide which things cannot be postponed. Is the request for the move of a desk to the other side of the room a logical request? If it is, rush changes then have to be made of the telephone and electric outlets and anything else affected by this change.

The designer must follow one cardinal rule: a true problem, like an irate client, does not just disappear when the designer turns his back. Problems and irate clients must be faced immediately. Any other course of action will anger the client and aggravate the already irritated situation. When something is wrong, the first thing to do is to correct it. After the client is satisfied that action has been taken, there will be plenty of time in which to search out the cause of the problem and affix the responsibility, financial or otherwise, for its correction. Never lose sight of the fact that you are rendering a service. The measure of your success will be the client's satisfaction with your ability to plan, to design, and to guard his money as though it were your own, and to do all this while keeping him as free from problems as possible.

The things to be done before, during, and after a move are described at the end of this chapter as Checklist K. The things that should have been done and were not become part of a list that should be prepared after the client has moved in. The purpose of this is to list things undone, as well as things the client may decide he needs. The first part of the **punch list,** prepared after a detailed inspection of the premises, will document the missing bulbs, hardware, switch plates, etc., as well as areas needing touch-up painting or repair because of damage caused by moving or damage due to last-minute construction.

The rapidity with which the contractor takes care of the finishing touches of a job can reflect very seriously on the designer's service, and you should do your utmost to see that these things are done as quickly as possible. Unfortunately, this can often be a very difficult thing to accomplish in a new building where there is one general contractor who works primarily for the landlord. Once the client has moved in and the landlord has begun to collect his rent, the general contractor moves his crew to the floors where the next tenant is due to move in, and all his effort is concentrated on getting that tenant into his space and collecting his rent. It can become a real problem to get the needed trades back to the client's space in order to get the little things done that will finish the job.

Sometimes difficult problems are solved very easily. After one client's space had been carefully inspected the president of the company called to complain that an electrical outlet, next to his desk, wasn't working. A call to the electrical contractor had a man over to examine the faulty outlet in short order. The contractor called to assure the designer that the outlet was now working, but on the following day the client called again to complain. Another call was made to the contractor, another electrician visited the job, and once again the contractor called to say that there was nothing wrong with the outlet.

On the next day it started all over again with another call from the client, now more than a little annoyed at the nonoperating outlet. This time the designer didn't call the contractor. Instead he went on a visit of inspection. He walked into the president's office and learned that a desk lamp plugged in to the outlet was not working.

It was almost as embarrassing for the designer as it was for the president, but all the telephone calls, all the electrician's time, all the president's time, and all the designer's time spent in correcting a fault in an outlet had been expended needlessly. There was no bulb in the lamp!

The second part of the punch list is made up of those things that the client, living in his new home, decides he now needs—things that he didn't think he would need despite the original checklist coverage, like extra shelving for the bookkeeper or message slots at the reception desk. The punch list should also include items he had originally thought would be unnecessary, like new furniture for the vice-president, whose old furniture, in new surroundings, suddenly looks shabby. The items on this part of the punch list should be treated as were the items on the checklist. Shelving should not merely be built but should be priced from prepared detail drawings and the building of them authorized by signature, just as all carpentry and cabinetwork were authorized initially. The vice-president's office should be budgeted and a design presented; when his furniture is approved, authorizations should be signed, purchase orders issued, and delivery scheduled just as it would have been had this item been part of the original design presentation. The fact that the remaining work is minor in comparison with the total job done is no reason to relax on any of the procedures previously used. The business of space planning and design is an exacting taskmaster. One of the quickest ways to disaster is to fail to follow any of the procedures that had been so carefully conceived as safeguards for you and for your client. The minutes that never get written, the authorizations that never get signed, and the purchase orders that never get checked will result in problems that will haunt you, no matter how perfect the rest of your efforts may have been.

CHECKLIST K   THE MOVE

This checklist includes all the things that must be done by the client, the mover, or the designer. The lists should be checked by management and designer early in the planning stage of the project, and the responsibility for the accomplishment of each item should be assigned. Schedules must be planned and target dates set, with the understanding that the planner is to watch job progress and keep the client advised about the ability to maintain the dates or the necessity for rescheduling them.

Some of the items on the list must be accomplished prior to the move, some during the move, and others after the move. Each must be done on time to facilitate the effectiveness of the overall schedule.

Checklist K
The Move

1. Choose company personnel to supervise the move at both the old and new headquarters.
   The moving company will supply its supervisory personnel, and the planner will act as a coordinator of the move.
2. Choose a company to handle the moving.
   Movers should be asked to bid, and each invited bidder should be supplied with a furniture plan. Bidders should be invited to tour the existing space, so that each may review the equipment that is to be relocated.
3. Schedule dates:
   (a) for weekend, weekday, or week-night move.
   (b) for dismantling and reassembling of special machinery and equipment that would be moved at a time different from the actual relocation time. This could include special sinks, water coolers, printing equipment, data-processing equipment, and anything else that would take more than normal moving time for dismantling and reassembling.
   (c) for refurbishing of furniture and equipment and its on-time delivery to the new offices.
   (d) for delivery of furniture and equipment being purchased.
4. Tag all furniture, equipment, and cartons, and check them off against the space planner's original inventory.
5. Code the final furniture plan with colors, numbers, and letters that coincide with the tagging.
6. Notify employees of the move and assign individual responsibility for the packing of individual equipment.
7. Keep employees aware of progress of construction at new quarters, and either arrange for tours just prior to move-in or provide each with a floor plan of his new area.
8. Arrange for moving notice to be sent to clients, suppliers, post office, banks, insurance companies, etc.
9. Schedule public relations effort, including plans for news releases, articles, "office-warming" parties, etc.
10. Order all necessary stationery such as letterheads, cards, forms, checks, etc.
11. Notify subscription lists, newspapers, magazines, etc., of new ad-

dress, and arrange for change of listing in telephone directories, trade papers, etc. Also arrange for listing on lobby directory of new building.
12. Schedule distribution of packing equipment such as boxes, crates, and bins, and schedule the actual packing.
13. Assignments should be made of personnel to supervise the removal work at the old premises.
14. Put up directional signs, room cards, and area labels in the new quarters.
15. Arrangements should be made for any required hoisting equipment.
16. Schedule the reinstallation of dismantled special machinery and equipment.
17. Arrange for telephone tie-in between the old and new offices to help with move coordination.
18. Schedule elevator service in both buildings.
19. Plan for adequate parking facilities at both locations and check arrangements, when necessary, with local police or traffic departments.
20. Obtain required permits for moving, parking, hoisting, etc.
21. Check adequacy of insurance coverage during the move.
22. Where necessary to protect property, special guards may have to be hired.
23. Protect elevator cabs, lobbies, walls, floors, etc., against damage from moving.
24. Arrange for a moving supervisor and moving headquarters in the new area.
25. Schedule staff work for getting files set up, supplies shelved, and all other unpacking accomplished that is necessary to the quick start of business operations right after the move.
26. Schedule telephone installers on standby duty to assure the correctness of all hookups and to take care of last-minute changes quickly, so that communications can be in operation when the offices open for business.
27. Arrange for cleaning after the move has been completed; all

boxes, cartons, bins, etc., should be removed from the premises as soon as possible.

28. The moving committee should schedule employees required to put desks in order and organize individual work areas. Tags and labels should be removed from furniture and equipment.
29. Moving committee or moving supervisor should check the inventory of items being moved, to make sure that everything has been delivered.
30. A lost-and-found department should be set up to locate lost equipment, fountain pens, etc.
31. A list of items to be completed by the contractors or delivered and installed by suppliers should be prepared by the planner and the items on it expedited by him. It is the planner's responsibility to see that all of these things are accomplished for the client.
32. Handle the design and procurement of additional items to be built or purchased, such as shelving, storage bins, an extra chair, etc.
33. Arrangements should be made for continued supervision and maintenance of the new quarters. Housekeeping responsibilities should be assigned, with rules set up to safeguard against any unwanted personal decoration attempts.

And now, even though the client is comfortably housed in the new offices you planned and designed for him, the exercise cannot be considered complete until the premises of the client's company have been examined.

Photos 1 to 3 are pictures of the offices of the ABC Corporation.

1. A view of the ABC Corporation secretarial area (2a) looking toward the mirrored wall of the reception room.

The ABC Corporation is not really the name of the company whose offices are here pictured nor did we truly describe the work of the company. The requirements are not accurate, the inventory was partially invented, and the tabulation of footage was as false as the rest. The secretarial area is the same, however, and so is the reception room. And an account of one of the rooms of the real company was used to describe the office of the ABC sales manager.

2. A closeup view of the reception room showing the glass divider wall of the reception room and the planters behind it.

3. A view of the sales manager's office.

The photographs shown on the following pages were chosen because each illustrates a specific contribution that design has made in meeting a functional requirement. With rare exception, the design solutions serve the prime need of all clients: to use space intelligently and without waste. Credits are indicated in the list of photographs on page 189.

OVERFILE STORAGE

The cost of renting or building space is calculated on a square foot basis. With the price per square foot going ever higher, the space planner had to find a way to utilize as many cubic feet above the floor surface as he could. Each piece of furniture and equipment that occupied floor space had to be examined in order to determine if some space-saving method for replacing it could be devised.

Photo 4 pictures cabinets above files. The material stored in the cabinets consists of forms, letterheads, envelopes, and other stationery used daily by the desk occupants. Previously, these items had been kept in two steel cabinets that had occupied 12 square feet of space and had required 24 square feet of aisle and work space.

Photo 5 illustrates the same principle of overfile storage in a smaller area.

6

OVERFILE WORK AREA

Each secretary in this executive secretarial area on Photo 6 required a work surface in addition to her desk. Since each also required two 4-drawer files, the work surface was provided as the top of two-drawer files. The actual space saved per secretary, without calculating aisle space, was 6-1/4 square feet.

Photo 7 illustrates the same principle of work surface above two-drawer files. In this case the files are recessed into the corridor wall. The file tops provide required work surfaces for each of the executive offices into which the files extend.

7

WALL-HUNG STORAGE

This illustrates another simple method to conserve floor space—the wall-hung cabinet. The cabinet hanging over a desk or other work surface allows you to place material within easy reach of the user. The offices shown are 42 square feet each. That such a small area could be used as an office is due in part to the use of the wall-hung storage cabinet.

UNDER-DESK STORAGE

The 48 square-foot office (8 feet by 6 feet) shown in Photo 9 provides L-shaped desk-top space along the 8- and 6-foot walls. The area accommodates two 42-inch conserva-files and a drawer pedestal with two small drawers and one file drawer. Shelf space 1 foot deep has been recaptured from the unused area under the desk of the cubicle behind this one. Two sets of hinged doors at the left give access to this shelf space.

10

11

OVERFILE PROJECTION ROOM

The client's request for a projection room adjacent to the conference room was met in rather unique fashion when further questioning revealed that the projection room was used only three or four times a year. It would have been a needless waste of space to devote major footage to a facility used so infrequently. The rear wall of the conference room separated it from the executive secretarial area. It was therefore decided to use the secretarial file wall for the projection equipment.

Photo 10 shows how the bank of five-drawer files (with overfile storage) was interrupted by the use of four 3-drawer files.

Photo 11 shows why. Two portholes in the conference room wall make it possible to project through one while the projectionist looks through the other. A small light over one of the portholes is a signal (given from the conference room) for the projectionist. One of the secretaries acts as projectionist.

STORAGE AREA AS SPACE DIVIDER

The two 5-drawer files, with the storage cabinet above, faces into a secretarial anteroom to an executive office. The white panel to the left of the files is the back of a similar two-file storage cabinet unit that faces the secretary to the next executive office. The white panel to the right of the files is a door to the coat closet, a closet accessible from the other side as well, and used by both secretaries and both executives.

SECRETARIAL CORRIDOR

Although the secretarial pools and the open work areas are both accepted principles of office planning, on occasion it is necessary to provide partial privacy for some secretaries. Photo 13 shows one way in which secretaries, with their desks placed in a corridor, were each given the feeling of having an individual work area. The divider separating each desk from the corridor is a 3-foot-wide panel. Photo 14, although not of the same area as that shown on Photo 13, is used in the same company's space. It illustrates how effectively the divider panel helps to give an organized appearance to what could be a very cluttered area.

AREA CONTROL

Because of the nature of the service business in which this client is engaged, it was necessary to plan the reception room so that it could be used twenty-four hours a day.

At the left side of Photo 15 is the reception desk at which the daytime receptionist sits. At night, the name panel slides back (Photo 16) and the girl at the switchboard behind it becomes the receptionist. In addition, she performs duties as telephone operator.

SELLING AREA

Photo 17 shows the classical sheet music department of a music store. The sale at the counter may be rapidly made or it may be made to a customer who, wishing to study the music before purchasing, may do so in comfort at a well-lighted, easeled space.

18

19

20

MULTIPLE-PURPOSE AREAS
Meeting Room - Lunch Room - Classroom

The meeting room (Photo 18) has cork-board display space and a chalkboard. The room next to it, separated by a folding wall, is used as a staff lunch room. With the folding wall open, the two rooms together serve as a classroom (Photo 19). The space behind the displays (Photo 20) is a storage area for extra chairs.

DUAL-PURPOSE AREAS
Office - Sitting Room - Conference Room

The combination room shown in Photo 21 can be separated into office-sitting room by closing the folding wood wall that rides in the ceiling and floor tracks. The sitting room serves as a conference room and the panel on the rear wall folds down to become the conference table. The table can also be used for product examination and is equipped with a mechanism that permits it to be adjusted in various tilt positions as shown on Photo 22.

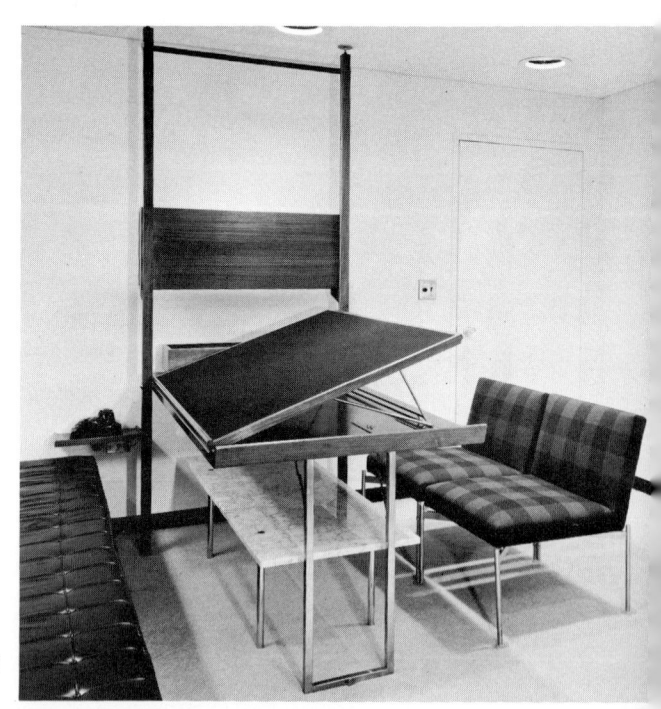

DUAL-PURPOSE ROOM
Conference Room

The conference room of an advertising agency must serve many purposes. It has to be a meeting room, a display room for graphics, and an audiovisual room. The long wall of Photo 23 is made up of a series of fabric-covered cork panels for pin-up display, plus a notched rail for easel display of board presentations. The far wall is wood panelled. Photo 24 shows how additional cork-covered panels can be drawn across the wood wall. A panel in the side wall is shown open to reveal a recessed television set.

DUAL-PURPOSE ROOM
Conference Room (cont.)

In Photo 25 the wood-panelled wall of Photo 23 is pulled back to show the projection screen behind it. The rear wall of the same conference room is the projection room wall. Photo 26 shows the viewing and projection ports of this wall.

27

DUAL-PURPOSE ROOM
Private Office - Meeting Room

The executive who occupies this office (Photo 27) requires a work station with an abnormally large amount of space for paper storage. His desk has four file drawers in addition to the wall-hung storage slots for file folders. He also has need for a drafting table.

Desk and drafting table can be concealed from the rest of the room (Photo 28) behind the panelled wall of doors at the rear. The executive is away from his office for many weeks of the year. If his desk area is closed off, his papers can remain undisturbed when others use his office for client meetings.

28

29

30

DUAL-PURPOSE ROOM
Board Room - Screening Room

This is the board room of a company that owns and operates a chain of motion-picture theaters. It was designed without the usual formal conference table in order to avoid the usual status distinctions attached to table seating. When in use for board meetings or staff conferences, this seating arrangement encourages the participants to communicate more freely. Photo 29 shows the room set up for such a meeting. When the room is to be used for screenings, the change is easily accomplished. Chairs swivel around and the teak panelling swings back to reveal a full-sized screen (Photo 30). Storage for extra chairs is concealed behind side panels. The center storage area contains full sound equipment for movie films.

31

DUAL-PURPOSE ROOM
Private Office - Meeting Room

This is a five-year-later version of an office for the same executive whose quarters were shown on Photos 27 and 28. When his company moved from one location to another, the same requirements had to be accommodated.
Photo 31 shows the office area completely open. The drafting board is parallel to the desk but hidden by the wall jog at the very right of the picture. Instead of using hinged doors to hide the desk area, a "roll-top room" was created (Photo 32) utilizing a garage-door mechanism to open or shut off the work space.

32

DUAL-PURPOSE ROOM
Conference Room - Display Room

Some conference rooms, unlike that of the advertising agency shown on Photos 23–26, require a great deal of display space for staff use and not for display to clients. Photo 33 illustrates how sliding cork panels, chalkboard, and storage area can be hidden behind hinged doors when display and demonstration facilities are not required.

COMPACT WORK AREA

These secretarial work areas were planned to meet multiple requirements. The seat to the left of the desk is for the use of personnel who must dictate reports of meetings as soon as they return to the office. Their phone messages are taken for them so that the secretaries do not waste time waiting for phone calls to be completed during dictation.

The pedestal to the right of the dictating seat is a file drawer. Stationery is kept in the pedestal (not shown) to the right and under the typewriter. To avoid giving up work space, the phone is hung from a cradle in the raised section above the desk. Phone dial, telephone control buttons, in-and-out baskets, supply section, and message slots are all part of the raised unit.

35

36

DESIGN DETAILS
Hidden Facilities

The private office is divided into three distinct work areas: the formal desk area, a conference table area, and a comfortable sitting area. Because many of the meetings held in this office (Photo 35) are lengthy ones, several service facilities were provided. Photo 36 shows how these were accommodated behind the wood-panelled wall at the side of the desk. Double doors swing into the office to provide access to a compact unit of range, sink, refrigerator, liquor storage, and wall-hung pantry cabinet. Another door swings away from the office into a private washroom.

DESIGN DETAILS
Elevator Corridor

The view of the elevator corridor shown in Photo 37 is taken from the main reception room area (not shown). The design problem was to provide an attractive entrance to the back area of office space. The solution arrived at was to utilize a marble panel framed to match the area panels between elevator doors. Photo 38 shows the detail of the panel and the concealed door behind it.

37

38

DESIGN DETAILS
Entrance Corridor

Because of the size of the floor, and the distance from elevators to entrance doors, it was decided to take advantage of the corridor for institutional display. Sculptured forms of molecules and chemical combinations were given a jewel-like appearance by placing each in a separate, clear plastic show window, dramatically lighted from inside. The gallery look was enhanced by a display of fine photographs. Because of the manner in which the displays were placed, visual interest in them was stimulated, helping to minimize the length of the corridor.

DESIGN DETAILS

The reception desk (Photo 40) was designed with a shelf raised above its surface so that mail and packages left at the desk would not interfere with the work going on there. Since marble was used on the panels behind the desk, a slab of marble was utilized as the desk shelf to protect against the daily abuses the shelf would normally receive.

Photo 41 illustrates the manner in which an unattractive standard office building facility is hidden from view.

PART II PLANNING FOR DESIGN

CHAPTER VI THE PRACTICE

Office planning and design, as it has been described in the previous chapters, is practiced in many ways by many different people with many different kinds of basic talents. Before discussing the personnel, procedures, and philosophies of the specialist in office planning and design, it would be well to describe briefly the various kinds of organizations that are involved in this work and their approaches to it.

The fact that reference is constantly made to "organization" is not meant to imply that office planning and designing can only be done by an organization. It can, in fact, be done by one man, twenty men, or one hundred men.

Whether the student reader wants to be part of a small or large organization or operate as a one-man business, he should want not only to understand the total effort that makes for a planning and designing job, from the initial selling effort to the final installation of the last switch plate, but also to know all about the variety of ways in which planning can be approached. ■

SECTION I THE PRACTICE OF OFFICE PLANNING

The top management of a company contemplating a move to new quarters interviewed a number of organizations involved in office planning and design. After several interviewing sessions, the chairman of the selection committee made the statement that, from what he had been able to learn after talking to so-called "practitioners," office planning was practiced by architects with a decorating department or decorators with an architectural department. This amusing, well-phrased statement was nevertheless a highly inaccurate one.

Prior to the introduction of air conditioning, space planning was concerned only with fitting the tenant into space whose shape was dictated by building codes that limited the distance from the nearest window. The architect's ability to design a building that could meet all the requirements of business was hampered by these same codes, so that companies renting space in multiple-occupancy office buildings had to adapt themselves to the shape of the space. Companies moving into their own buildings used their own talents, or that of their architect, for this fitting process.

As office renting became more competitive, some of the real estate companies began to use design and architectural services to prove to potential tenants that they could fit into the space being offered to them. But the whole effort was rather haphazard, and it was still a fitting process rather than a planning one.

In the 1930s (when design became important in the competitive product market), the country as a whole, led by the business community and the industrial designers, became more design-conscious. Newly designed products and packages required freshly designed showrooms, and the new showrooms pointed up the shabbiness of the business office. A few designers, involved with building design, product design, and display design, were suddenly exposed to the design of business interiors and learned how inefficiently American business was using the space it rented. It was at this point that the companies who have given major impetus to the whole field of space planning and design were born: the companies whose sole reason for being is office planning and design. This planning effort was not made by the architect with the decorating department or the decorator with the architectural department, but by the office planner. A few had practiced architecture, a few had been product designers, and others had been involved in various design fields ranging from scenic design to department-store-display design. But they all had one thing in common: a consuming interest in planning and designing efficient, attractive homes for business in space whose previously limited boundaries had been widened by the technical advances of the building industry.

This is not meant as editorializing. It is meant to point up the strength of the space-planning effort. It is an aid to business in the proper utilization of the space it occupies, as well as an aid to architecture in validating the buildings the architect designs. Whether the planner be architect, interior designer, industrial designer, or whatever, he must be vitally interested in the work that goes on at a secretarial desk. If he is not, he should not be an office space planner.

Space planning, in one form or another, is practiced by many different kinds of companies. A brief description of some of these efforts follows. The organization of the company specializing in office planning and design is described in the next chapter, along with the individual talents that are utilized there.

The Office Furniture Dealer

As a rule, the office furniture dealer offers a very limited service geared to help a customer buy new things for a private office he is furnishing. The staff usually consists of a draftsman or an interior designer who can draw and who doubles as a floor salesman when there is nothing to be done on his drawing board. He will work out color schemes and coordinate furniture and fabric selections for old and new customers. His work is usually confined to small jobs and is always limited to the selection of those items of furniture, furnishings, and accessories that are handled by the dealer. There is no fee for this service. The dealer considers it an aid to sales. It is a helpful service arm to office furniture dealers but does not truly fill the role of office planner and designer as defined in this text.

The Office Furniture Manufacturer

A few manufacturers of office furniture have formed their own planning departments. Originally started as service arms to help their furniture customers with space-planning problems, these departments have been extended and offered as independent services. They are, of course, anything but independent, specifying only the furniture they manufacture and not necessarily the furniture and equipment that will best fit the job to be done.

Usually there is no separate fee for this service given by the furniture manufacturer. The actual design fee is, instead, represented by the difference between the list and net price of the furniture sold.

The Interior Decorator

The interior decorator's service is usually only a little broader than the service offered by the office furniture dealer. He is concerned with furnishing rooms, the architectural aspects of which have already been determined. He differs from the dealer because he makes available to the client whatever line or piece of furniture, furnishings, or accessories he thinks is right for the job, and he is not confined to a manufacturer or a limited number of manufacturers. This, however, is also not truly a space-planning effort but a furnishings one, with little or no interest shown in the problems of organizational layout and little or no concern with operating efficiency. The service is generally paid for by a fee calculated as a percentage of the cost of the furniture specified.

The Interior Designer

Most interior designer's service is the same as that offered by interior decorators. It is only recently that interior design schools have begun to include basic planning courses in their curricula that make it possible for the interior designer to include some planning in his service. Despite these advances, the interior designer's training is involved mainly with colors and styles and fabrics, and not with the probing and searching and understanding of the things that go on within the office, and the necessity to translate the operational needs of a company to the realities of the space it will occupy.

The Industrial Designer

The industrial designer is trained as a designer of products and packaging and displays. His is an understanding of the materials used in the manufacture of a product and the mechanical processes used in that manufacturing. His approach to product design entails the same detailed study of function which marks the effort of the office planner. Although the industrial designer designs for business and is constantly concerned with the merchandising and salability of the product he designs, his major interest is not the business office itself or the individual work stations which, added together, make up the total business operation.

The Architect

For most architects, office planning is not a primary effort. Those who specialize in office planning and design and who do little or no building design really fall into the category described in the next chapter dealing with the office planner and designer.

The office planning work of the architect is usually confined to the building planned for individual occupancy, and even then very little interest is shown in the individual work stations that dictate the purpose of the building. Those firms that do design multiple-occupancy buildings usually have no interest in handling the tenant work and little interest in the space studies that are done for landlord or real estate agents as part of the renting program.

Very few architects get involved in planning offices in multiple-occupancy buildings, but those few who do handle tenant work have usually set up special divisions within their own organizations or, as in the case of one architectural firm, set up a separate corporation with its own trade name.

The architect's training, like that of the industrial designer or the engineer, is a specialized one. Up to now, it has not included the details of business office needs, built as the business offices are around the work stations of the individual employee. If the architect is to become interested in the field of office planning, he must be prepared to devote his time to learning new talents in order to do justice to this new specialty.

CHAPTER VII ORGANIZING THE COMPANY

Knowledge of the procedural steps described in the first five chapters of this book will not guarantee the successful completion of a planning project. To this knowledge must be added the important ingredients that will help make your own effort run smoothly—the efficient operation of the design company.

To do justice to your claim for rendering service you must be prepared to protect the client from undue concern not only about your ability to plan and design, but about your ability to properly administer all the details of his project. Your organizational know-how must be reflected by all your people and in everything you do.

The people who work for you, the procedures they follow, and the underlying philosophy of your business activities are part of your image. You must be good planners, you must be good designers, but if you are to convince a potential client that you are capable of understanding his organization, you had better have yours in good working order. ■

SECTION I ORGANIZING THE COMPANY PERSONNEL

To be a good space planner and designer requires interest and knowledge of business, design, architecture, drafting, furniture, fabrics, etc. The personnel records of office planning companies reveal that employees come from such varied training as industrial engineers, mechanical engineers, office managers, architects, industrial designers, furniture salesmen, architectural draftsmen, interior designers, management consultants, scenic designers, display designers, sculptors, and even cartoonists.

The office planner, although in a field that usually takes second billing to the architect who designed the building, nevertheless wants to be a space planner because the curiosities and talents and goals that are part of space planning add up to his idea of life interest and fulfillment. His satisfaction stems from the preparation of the initial program that gives validity to the single-occupancy building, from the contribution of his knowledge of business-space use to the initial planning of the multiple-occupancy building, and from the increase he effects for the efficiency of the business office plus the improvement he brings to the environment of the people who work there.

As a design company grows and needs more help it comes face-to-face with the hiring-and-firing problems of any service business. Hiring because of an immediate need for help in turning out a sudden influx of work can only lead to firing when the panic subsides. Any office that follows a practice of easy hiring and easy firing quickly gains a reputation in the field and soon finds it difficult to attract competent help. Hiring should be done only when job projections show that new people can be kept on for a long period of time. If this does not seem possible, it is far better to take care of a sudden influx of work by allowing your present staff to work overtime until the extra jobs are completed.

The personnel list of any office may consist of one name or one hundred names. No matter how large the payroll, the tasks to be accomplished are basically the same in every organization. The purpose of this chapter is to describe those tasks. The size of each design organization will dictate how the work will be divided.

Each job falls under one of two headings: production and administration. Production-personnel time, directly connected with actual projects, can be charged to those specific projects for each hour spent on that project during the working day. Administrative-personnel time is not directly chargeable to specific projects. Administrative effort is involved in all the projects and with general company work. Each job description that follows has been listed under its appropriate heading. The specific production jobs are listed first, followed by the production supervisory categories that would be required in the larger design organizations. What follow are job descriptions but not descriptions of the whole job. What each person does in the implementation of a project can be best understood by studying each job effort, along with the company procedures outlined in the next section and the project procedures of Chapters I–V.

Production

1. Project Director. This is the man directly responsible for guiding a project from its inception to its conclusion. He arranges and attends all meetings and coordinates the production of the job. It is to him that the client must turn for information, and it is he who must interpret and explain to the client all that is being done on the job. He asks the questions, gets the answers, and writes the reports. He should prepare a condensed version of the client work letter for use by the estimator, designer, and technical draftsman for their reference in checking the work to be done. He oversees the space analysis and the space study and works with the estimator on the budget. He consults with the designer as the design presentation is prepared and with the expediter on the preparation of authorization forms. He conducts the meeting at which designs are presented and explains all details of design to the client at this meeting. He is available to work with the technical draftsmen as they complete the working drawings, and he checks their work for errors of commission or omission before the drawings are sent out for bidding. He helps with the letting of contracts and with the ordering of furniture, furnishings, and accessories. He and the technical draftsmen check shop drawings. During the course of construction, he makes periodic visits to the site to observe the progress of the job and to report on the quality of the work. He approves contractor's progress billing. When the tenant is ready to occupy the space, the project director is present for the move and helps to see that all goes smoothly before, during, and after it. It is his responsibility to prepare (usually with the help of the field supervisor) the list of things still to be done after the client occupies his new premises and then to see that they get done quickly. His final responsibility is the approval of all bills as each phase of the work is satisfactorily completed.

2. Space Analyst. It is the job of the space analyst to translate the operational requirements into a study of the space the client intends to occupy. He works closely with the project director while he prepares his rough sketches and his final study. It is his responsibility to do or arrange to have done any required field checks, in order to make sure that his studies are done on the most accurate plans available. The space analyst does all the measurements of plans and the computation of rentable and usable footage. He must be thoroughly familiar with local building codes, so that his studies are not in violation of their requirements. Since speed is often required if the space-study effort aids a renting program, the space analyst must be prepared to work rapidly and to keep accurate scheduling records.

3. Designer. The designer attends the initial design meeting and subsequently works with the estimator in the preparation of the preliminary budget. This requires broad design decisions that can be defined after the budget has been approved. The designer will make recommendations for space-study changes that may become necessary in order to achieve design goals. He will work out the furniture layouts of areas that are to be specially designed and develop the sketches and color schemes that will be submitted for internal critiques. His sketches will show materials, furniture, finishes, etc., that have been selected within the dollar framework of the budget. After the sketches have been studied and final decisions made, the designer will prepare the plans, drawings, renderings, and design boards for the design presentation. He will work with the estimator on the preparation of the budget that will be presented with the design and with the expediter on the preparation of authorizations for client signature. He will attend the design presentation, he will be prepared to explain the designs, and he will take notes on the details of any agreed changes.

After approval of the design, he will work on the rough sketches of the details of any design. The details will then have to be prepared by the technical draftsmen as part of the working drawings. The designer will be available for consultation and to make any required changes as the job progresses. He will also be available for interpretation of any cabinetwork shop drawings and to help the field supervisor with any design changes that he may be called upon to make because of field conditions.

4. Estimator. This is the man responsible for the preparation of the budget and the revisions that may be made to it. It is up to him to keep voluminous up-to-date records on unit costs of all things connected with the building and the outfitting of office space. Sometimes the estimating job is divided between two people; one is responsible for construction and installation items and the other is responsible only for furniture, furnishings, carpets, drapes, and accessories. The one who estimates the cost of furniture (sometimes also the expediter) is responsible for obtaining day-to-day information on the availability and cost of furniture, fabrics, carpets, etc. He will keep catalogs and price lists up to date and provide information to the design-department sample room for the retirement of samples of discontinued numbers.

5. Technical Draftsman. The technical draftsman prepares all the plans that make up the set of working drawings. He works closely with the project director and consults with him on all questions and problems. He works from the inventory and draws the furniture, telephone, and electrical plan. His drawing of the telephone conduit is done in conjunction with the telephone company representative. The reflected ceiling plan is worked out with the designer and with the help of the engineering performance chart of the specified fixture, so that the light output is properly calculated. He prepares the partition plan, the paint and flooring plan, the construction and cabinet details, and all the schedules and legends that are part of the drawings. It is his job, too, to check any shop drawings and schematic air-conditioning-duct drawings to assure their conformity with overall plans. In addition to working with the project director, he will consult with the designer concerning design elements that must be detailed.

6. Field Supervisor. The field supervisor visits each job daily to guide and to work with the contractor. He must be thoroughly familiar with all aspects of the plans and the schedules to be met, and he must see to it that the contractor adheres to the schedules. He must keep the office aware of any problems and any possible interference with the schedule.

Job changes or additions should be accomplished only through him, and he should obtain any change costs that are needed. He must make certain that job changes are reported to the technical draftsman, so that all plans are kept constantly up to date. Should a supervisory progress chart be required, he will maintain one for office use and for transmittal to the client. He will help the project director when the client moves into the space and will, with the project director, prepare the punch list of items requiring attention.

7. Production Head. The production head has the responsibility of **scheduling** a project through to completion, of assigning the personnel required to complete it, and of making certain that the schedules are maintained. In addition, he has the responsibility for the smooth operation of the production facilities, including the reproduction of drawings, production of reports, keeping central production files up to date, and maintaining the samples, catalogs, and production library. He must give general consulting help in rearranging assignments to meet the day-to-day problems that may arise. He must provide drafting or site-checking aid for any other department needing this kind of help. He must also be available to supply project information for the accounting department that will help them in their progress billing.

8. Project Coordinator. The project coordinator works with the production head in providing project director personnel for each project, and he consults with him when each project is scheduled. He helps the project director carry out his work and discusses and helps him with project problems. He attends design meetings, and has sufficient client contact so that he will be accepted as a project-director substitute when it is impossible for the project director to be present at any job meeting. His day-to-day familiarity with each project through the study of minutes and his regularly scheduled meetings with each project director makes it possible for him to help with whatever problems arise. He is in charge of distributing the plans to contractors for their bidding purposes and, after the client has chosen the contractor who will do the work, he is responsible for notifying the bidders. He receives the field supervisor's reports and the expediter's report and acts upon any problems that each may be having.

9. Technical-drafting Coordinator. This is one of the few supervisory jobs responsible for project production. The technical-drafting coordinator, with the production head, the project coordinator, and the design coordinator, arranges the scheduling of each project. He assigns **technical-drafting department** personnel, maintains the schedules of each job, and checks, or arranges to have checked, all drawings, shop drawings, and engineering schematics. The personnel of his department must be available to help with field checking and inventory taking.

10. Design Coordinator. The design coordinator supervises the work of the **design department** and assigns design personnel to each project. He helps each designer with the problems of design, detailing, and budget. He will attend the design meetings with the client and the designer, and he will make certain that all design schedules are being maintained. He is responsible for the design sample room, the preparation of design presentations, and the file of past design presentations.

Administration

1. Project Developer. This is a task that, in some design companies, is a production job rather than an administrative one. It is being considered here as effort put forth mainly by the principals of a design company whose time is not usually accounted for as chargeable to a specific project. The prime function of the developer is to carry out the first phase of problem solving. Because no project can advance beyond the first phase until the initial report and space study prove that a move or change is feasible, the first part of the developer's work is basically a sales effort. He will meet with the client, gather all the information necessary to understand the problem, and guide the planning effort from the acceptance of the space study through whatever building or renting arrangements have to be made to get the project launched and into the hands of the project director.

2. Expediter. The job defined herein is concerned only with furniture and furnishings, rather than any construction effort. Within that framework, the expediter is responsible for the pricing of furniture and furnishings, the preparation of the forms authorizing their purchase, the purchase orders that are sent to the manufacturer and dealers, as well as the programming and policing of the schedule for manufacture and delivery. It is the expediter's job, guided by the schedules supplied to him by project director and supervisor, to arrange for the on-time delivery of all purchased items.

3. Controller. The controller is in charge of all financial aspects of the business and will maintain a staff the size of which will be dictated by the paper work handled by his department. He is responsible for billing and bill collecting, for bookkeeping and tax paying, for the administration of all employee benefit plans, and for reporting to the principals, at agreed-upon periods, upon the state of the financial health of the company. It is his job to attend to the necessary paper work that is required to please the Internal Revenue Service, the state and city governments, and the banking community. Most important of all is the role he must play in keeping management constantly advised of its projected future.

4. Management. Large organizations will require people in management capacities to handle tasks that are extensions of production and administration efforts. These are basically coordinating jobs concerned with the smooth running of the operation and with overall client relations. The jobs defy simple description since each is born because of an evolved necessity for its creation.

5. Management Services

(a) Secretaries. Secretarial help will be required for the typing of minutes of meetings, client requirements, reports, proposals, contracts, and general correspondence. The number of secretaries will be determined by the activity of each design office.

(b) Filing. This covers the filing of drawings (both plans and design-department drawings), samples, job folders, accounting files, etc. Filing can be handled by secretaries, the office boy, the head of the print department, or by personnel hired specifically for this work.

(c) Print-department Head. The operation of print-making equipment (blueprint, mimeograph, copying machines, etc.) is usually done by the same person responsible for the orderly handling of deliveries, mail, supplies, and print filing, in addition to report printing and binding. The size of his department and the number of people assisting him will, of course, depend on the size of the design office. Office-boy activities and office-maintenance chores are usually his responsibilities also.

Organizing the Company Procedures

SECTION II   ORGANIZING THE COMPANY PROCEDURES

It would be best to describe the details and procedures with which every design office must become involved in the order of exposure to them during the conduct of a particular project.

The first item in project exposure is the **contract,** without which there is no project. The review of a contract which follows is no encroachment on the prerogatives of the legal profession, nor will the designer's adherence to the paragraphs concerning financial record keeping automatically entitle him to become a certified public accountant. The designer will need the help of both professions, but both professions must be guided by the designer's experiences.

The contract can be as formal in verbiage or as informal as each designer and his attorney wish it to be. It should provide sufficient safeguards for both designer and client so that they can start a project with mutual trust.

The contract must be a clearly stated document that adequately describes all phases of the design effort. It should, as closely as possible, outline the procedures to be followed in chronological order: the space study, design meeting, budgeting, inventory taking, design presentation, working drawings, etc. It should describe the required coordination of mechanical plans and the process of securing and letting contracts for the work to be done. It should describe the extent of progress reporting as well as the help to be given in the installation of furniture and furnishings.

The contract must outline the **fee** structure and the provisions for progress payments or time-charge billing. It should carry paragraphs providing for reimbursement of out-of-pocket expenses, travel expenses, filing fees, and print costs, plus payment for work caused by client changes after original approval had been given. Finally it should specify how any claims or differences of opinion are to be adjudicated.

Contracts are prepared in many different forms. Some designers present theirs as typewritten documents, believing that this makes them more personal and is indicative of the personal effort that goes into each project. They sell their effort on this basis and constantly try to reflect this attitude.

Other designers believe that a printed contract form is the reflection of an established operation backed by the kind and quantity of experience that would be desirable to most clients. Even among the printed-form advocates there is a difference of opinion. Some favor blank spaces left in the body of the contract for the insertion of fees. Others work out the variations of fee structure in advance and print them in the contract, drawing a line through any nonapplicable fee sentences. The second group feels that this helps to establish the fee as a fixed price not subject to negotiation and thus enhances the reputation of the designer. This group believes that any odd or unusual situations can be covered by a typed addendum to the contract.

The fee, although included in the contract, requires separate discussion. A fee charged by any service business is based on the time spent on behalf of the client. Ideally the client would pay the salary of all personnel working on his job for the time they actually spend on it, plus a proportionate share of the overhead, rent, telephone, payroll taxes, etc., of the design company, and a percentage of the total of both amounts as profit. Many service companies, such as designers, architects, and engineers, compute this as $2\frac{1}{2}$ or 3 times the hourly payroll cost of the individuals involved in the project.

Despite the fact that it would be ideal to have the client pay solely on the basis of time spent on his job, it is only rarely that a client will accept this arrangement and only rarely that the designer will offer it. If they should agree on this kind of fee measurement, it is usually after they have had several project experiences with each other and after they have found out how well they can work together. Most clients prefer a measure of payment that will come as close to a fixed amount of money as possible. This can be x number of cents per square foot of area planned and designed, y percent of the dollars spent on the job, or some combination of x and y. In some instances it can even be x and y or $2\frac{1}{2}$ to 3 times payroll, whichever is the lesser.

The x number of cents per square foot usually constitutes a part or all of the fee when there is no cost of the job involved. This covers the work in preparing a tabulation of footage required, an evaluation report, a space study, a furniture plan, etc., and can even cover the preparation of plans for construction work that is to be done for a tenant at no cost to him. This would be true particularly where the work is done by a landlord as part of the lease arrangement.

In order to arrive at the value of x, the designer, plus financial advisory help, must be able to approximate the number of man-hours required for the job. He must then calculate the cost of those man-hours, plus overhead, plus profit, in order to arrive at a fixed fee, or he must divide the fixed fee by the footage to be studied so that x equals the number of cents per square foot that is to be charged to the client.

The percentage of cost represented by y becomes a measure of the fee, or a part of the fee, when dealing with an unknown amount of work. For example, when entering into a contract for planning and designing a client's offices, neither the client nor the designer can have any idea of the amount of effort that will go into the design of cabinetwork or the selection of fabrics, furniture, carpeting, etc. It is necessary therefore that the designer once again approximate the time that will be involved in this effort and equate that with a percentage of the cost of those items, so that he will be repaid for the man-hours (plus overhead, plus profit) required to design and select. The y percent is used not only to cover the design aspect of each job, but also to compensate for any part of the work measurable as a job cost to the client. This percentage can be the total fee when there is no contribution of work on the part of the landlord, or it could represent the total fee for work done for a company building for its own use, as well as for a company whose space is being rehabilitated. Exactly what y stands for in numbers will depend on the total amount of money expended by the client. It can, and has, varied from 5 to 20 percent.

The preparation of the space study represents the first part of project effort. The space study operation, if it is to run smoothly, requires careful record keeping. Each owner or rental agent of each new building erected will supply the designer with a brochure, rental plans, and a rental schedule showing the rentable footage available in the building for each floor. A file, or files, containing all this information should be kept for each building. As studies are done, the usable and rentable footage information for each of the completed studies should go into the appropriate building file.

In addition, a separate job file should be kept, filed by client name or job number for each space study and revision of studies done for that client. The footage calculation for each study should also go into that job file.

If the design office is involved in doing studies paid for by the building owner, it is quite possible that many studies may be prepared for each floor before that floor is finally rented. Rather than prepare original cores for each study, one original drawing should be made for each floor and then reproduced in transparency form for each study. By keeping a card record of each core prepared, it will be easy to quickly check on core availability.

A busy office will have a busy space-study department, and work in that department should be carefully scheduled. A schedule form carrying pertinent information such as **job number,** building studied, square feet involved, required completion date, actual completion date, and delivery date can, when periodically given to the accounting department, serve also as an aid to billing.

The job number mentioned before is very much a part of the record keeping for all departments and is usually used as the job identification on all production-personnel **time slips.** The numbers assigned should be recorded in a number book by the secretary in charge of sales activity or by the person in charge of space studies. The job number should be recorded on the contract, accounting folder, job file, space-study file, design file, estimating file, technical-drafting file, presentation drawings, bills, minutes, correspondence, bids, authorizations, purchase orders, and change orders.

The project director keeps complete **job files.** They should be separated into the components of job records—minutes of meetings, correspondence, budgets, bids, bills, and purchase orders, etc. Even though other people in the designer's office, in addition to the project director, may have correspondence and communication with the client, a copy of every written communication and of every memo covering verbal communications with the client should go to the project director for inclusion in his job file.

The condensed version of the work letter, prepared by the project director for distribution to budgeting, design, and technical drafting, should also be part of this file.

The minutes of meetings, in addition to being distributed to client personnel and to being included in the project-director file, should go to

Organizing the Company Procedures

each production department involved in any of the work outlined in the minutes themselves and to whatever supervisory and administrative personnel may be concerned with the project. The minutes must serve not only as safeguard for both client and designer, but also as a document of internal communication for the design office. Set up so that each category of effort is clearly indicated and easily culled from the body of the text, the minutes should be instruction sheets for each department. For example, if a particular set of minutes deals with things concerning the design department and the field supervisor, copies would be routed to each so that each could then take action on his particular aspect of the work.

The estimator will keep his own file of job costs, with an up-to-date listing of all prices kept according to trades. These trade subdivisions should reflect all the price information available, including the unit costs charged by as many different contractors and subcontractors as he can collect. His catalog of price information should also include, if possible, the credit and substitution allowances that appear in various leases, so that his budgets can properly reflect these allowances.

The design department must take care of samples, furniture and furnishings, and catalogs, as well as maintain its own job records. The samples should be as complete a collection of available material as can be gathered together. This would include hard and soft floor coverings, wall coverings, drapery and upholstery fabrics, glass, wood, synthetics, metals, etc. The samples should be kept readily available to the designers. It should be made a simple matter for the designer to easily and quickly examine complete lines of any product desired. Unless such viewing is made easy, many jobs will end up with the same carpet simply because that particular carpet sample happens to be at the top of the barrel. These samples should be backed up by a sufficient number of duplicates to allow for their inclusion on the design boards discussed in Chapter IV. The catalogs of furniture and furnishings should include all items currently in the line. Manufacturers and dealers will supply duplicate pictures of their merchandise so that they, too, can be made part of the design presentation.

A duplicate collection of catalogs and price lists should be kept by the person in charge of budgeting and ordering the furniture and furnishings.

It is important that all samples, catalogs, and price lists be kept up to date. Specifying and getting approval to purchase a particular fabric only to find out that it has been discontinued can be almost as disconcerting for the client as would be a rise in the price of an item that had already been approved at a lower cost. While on the subject of catalogs and sample keeping, it would be well to deal with the ever-present planner problem of keeping continually abreast of all that is new and available. He must know what is new in materials such as metals, woods, glass, plastics, and fabrics. He must be aware of the new furniture on the market, the new furnishings, the telephone systems that are being offered, the new files, copy machines, lighting fixtures, switch plates, hardware, etc. There are no limits to the things he should know about, and the only reason for frustration over the unending task of staying in the know would be the problem of finding time to do so. Catalogs and samples for the design department, catalogs and textbook library for the technical department, plus a general library of books and trade magazines for all personnel, will help considerably to get information spread about. Allowing salesmen to show their wares periodically, planned trips to factories and showrooms, as well as visits to the sites of jobs under construction, will also help to keep a staff aware of the new things that are on the market. The department supervisors should be urged to have occasional staff meetings, the purpose of which would be to bring new concepts to the attention of all personnel.

Job-design records would be kept by the designer assigned to the project. He would, with the project director, the design supervisor, and personnel from management, attend the first design meeting with the client and all subsequent meetings dealing with design. His records would include his own notes taken during the meetings as well as those project director's minutes which deal with design. They would also contain his design-development sketches, budget information with which he is concerned, and duplicates of the detail sketches he has prepared for the technical draftsman. These details show his solutions for the manufacture of items he has designed. They will be turned over to the technical draftsman so that they can be included on the drawings submitted to the contractors for bidding and building.

Photographs, in print or slide form, should be made of all design presentation boards after their completion. For one reason or another, presentation boards have a way of disappearing and a record of each presentation must be retained in the design office.

The technical-drafting department, the field supervisor, the expediter, and the estimator will each keep a job file in which will be retained project information pertinent to that particular effort. At the completion of the job, all job folders, including the project director's folder and the accounting folder, should be combined into one, with all duplicate pages destroyed. The file of plans should also be reduced after the completion of the project. Only original plans should be kept in order to cut down on what could otherwise become an impossible bulk of retained paper.

The scheduling of job effort immediately after the design meeting and again after the budget meeting should be done with all of the supervisory and administrative personnel involved in the project. This scheduling is important because it is necessary to know what the manpower availability is for conducting the project. The schedule is valueless unless it is followed, and it will be followed only if it is adequately policed. This policing becomes more important as you handle more and more projects with more and more people. Your commitment to the client for the delivery of plans to the landlord (or any other kind of commitment) started at the beginning of your effort. You will not meet it unless you have adhered to all the interim dates scheduled to help you keep that ultimate commitment. If the space study is not done on schedule you will delay all the effort that follows it. Schedules, therefore, must not only be planned in as much detail as possible but each detail of that schedule must be monitored constantly. It is also vitally important that production effort be measured and planned against the fee for the work. After the budget has been approved, the designer will have a fairly accurate idea of what the total fee will be for the project. By working backward from this fee, he can determine the number of hours that ideally should be used for each phase of the job. It should be possible to assign hours to the project director, designer, technical drafting, estimator, etc., based on the percentage of time that each will require on the project measured against the dollars that are available for that time and the hourly rate schedule computed for each kind of job effort.

This scheduling is, of course, planned for the ideal project that can be kept within the confines of the hours and dollars allotted to it. Sometimes more time is spent on one aspect of the work than was anticipated, but is balanced by using less time on another phase. Not all projects will return the same percentage of profit. In fact not all projects will be profitable, but unless the designer attempts to follow a schedule as closely as possible, he may never make a profit.

The accounting department plays an important role in helping to measure profit by activating and constantly updating a system of **job-cost analysis.** The accuracy of fee structures should be tested against job costs and changed to assure proper profit whenever job-cost history indicates inadequate returns.

The scheduling of personnel is important for other than the financial aspects of each project. It is necessary to help determine the availability of staff, the length of time until present personnel will be free for new work, and the necessity for adding to the staff to take care of an increase of contracted work.

Here again the controller and his department must play an important role. A design company can be successful only if it can properly manage its own affairs as effortlessly as possible, confining most of its energy to the business of planning and design. No service company can survive if it holds on to nonproductive employees too long or delays in hiring people to handle its full work load. The controller must do much to supply the information necessary to avoid both situations.

One way in which the accounting department helps to police the schedule is through time slips on which should be reported how every hour of production-personnel time was spent and on which job. Utilized to the fullest, the time slips will provide a necessary measure of the progress of a job, the basis for cost accounting completed jobs, and a historic background of past performance by category of work that will help in determining the fees to be asked on future job proposals.

The form of time reporting is an accounting problem and will vary according to the manner in which the accounting department keeps its time records. Some designers prefer to keep one sheet for each individual, with an entire week's work recorded in hourly or half-hourly increments. Others prefer to have each staff member keep a separate weekly sheet for each job he works on, no matter how many or how few hours he spent on it during the week. Many design firms are using the data-processing facilities of their accounting firm or bank for their record keeping. The important aspect of time reporting is that it be as accurate as possible, reflecting each person's time spent on each job and the kind of work done on the job. It will be helpful in cost accounting to be able to separate the time spent on each job into project-director time, estimator time, designer time, report-preparation time, etc. The more categories of effort that can be accurately shown the more precise future scheduling and future pricing will be.

By far the most difficult thing in time record keeping, whether the records are filled out with a quill pen or keypunched for IBM computers, is getting them filled out at all. There are always some in a design office to whom record keeping is anathema. Like it or not, however, it is a most necessary function and each office will have to devise its own method of coping with the non-record keepers. Ideally time slips should be turned in daily, in order to assure the greatest amount of accuracy. Too often time records that are collected once a week or once every two weeks are filled in at the last moment and can represent hazy memories, at best.

The time records, combined with progress reports on the percentage of completion of each project, will be vital in determining progress billing. Bills should be rendered monthly, covering time spent during the month or covering the percentage of job progress accomplished. They should also reflect any out-of-pocket expenses incurred for the client and any charges for prints that have been made. Designers, like most people in service businesses, tend to be lax in their billing habits. The businessmen for whom they work are not lax and will have greater respect for the designer who runs his operation in mature fashion. No design firm can operate unless it is paid, and paid promptly, for its effort.

SECTION III   ORGANIZING THE COMPANY PHILOSOPHY

Planning and designing have now been discussed from your first exposure to a problem through to its solution. The nature of the talent practicing planning and designing and the organization and procedures necessary for that practice have been thoroughly examined. One thing remains to be discussed: the individual direction in which each of you is to go.

Will your future be with a small design studio or a large design firm? Will this business belong to one man or many? Will you hang up your

Planning for Design

coat in the morning and put it back on again at night having done nothing except the work at hand, having learned nothing but the specifics of the project on the board? Are you to be motivated by your own curiosities and drives, in concert with those of the people with whom you work, or do you work feeding the drives and curiosities of others?

There is no one answer that could possibly be satisfactory for all of you. Each of you must search out his own way of life, and each must determine the character of the company he will keep.

Talk of the character of a design company is talk of the attitudes and philosophies that motivate the planning organization and the environment within which it functions. None of this is chartable, nor are there procedures or checklists that will help you make your decisions. What your organization is going to be like is up to you. The reputation it enjoys for the service it renders and the ethics it practices will be a reflection of what you put into its composition and what you expect to take from it.

You, who will help clients create the image they will present to their public, must surely create your own image with precise clarity. Everything you do must be indicative of what you want to do and what your talent will allow you to do. Your office, your stationery, your reports, and even the bills you send out must look as though each is the product of a design company. If you expect to sell your design talent you must display it at all times, whether your office be large or small, expensively or inexpensively furnished. Within your financial abilities, your environment must mirror and inspire you. No client who visits must ever do so without being thoroughly aware of the fact that these are the offices of a design company. Nothing that you do, nothing that you live and work with, nothing that you show to the public should ever proclaim anything but your consuming interest in planning and designing.

The graphics used must reflect this design interest and should, in fact, form a continuity of image that will be recognizable to clients at all times. Starting with the sign on your door, the title box on your plans, the identification on your renderings, and even the logo on your checks, this design theme—your theme—should carry through on everything you do. It is not enough, however, to be content only with the design of your letterhead. You must be just as critical of the letter that gets typed on it as you are of the letterhead itself. Poorly planned margins, badly composed letters, and sloppy typing will all help to defeat whatever positive design impression you may be trying to create. Your proposals must be perfect, your reports a model of organization, your presentations as graphically clear as possible. You are a designer. Everything you do must prove that fact.

There should be nothing forced about this reflection of design interest. It must be as natural for you to want this kind of perfection in yourself as it is for you to want to attain it for your client. Unless you have this interest in all details of design and in your lives as designers, it would be well to closely reexamine your motives for wanting a career in design. For that career will be short-lived if your interest is not a sincere one.

No creative effort is worthy to be called that if it is not honestly conceived. That is as true of planning and design as it is of painting or writing or composing. A surface cleverness or a charlatan approach may suffice for a project or two, but it will not survive as the foundation for a future.

This same sincerity, so necessary in design itself, must be equally apparent when you describe your design service to a potential client. As with any service, it is best explained by those who have been intimately connected with the production of that service.

The knowledge you bring to your effort and the way in which you use that knowledge will be reflected in the relationships you establish with the client. As in many service businesses, a recommendation from a client, happy with what has been done for him, is the designer's most satisfying source of new business. This source of business is not easy to come by, because it calls for perfection on the part of the designer in many facets of his work. To be so recommended his planning must be without fault, his design the proper admixture of interpretation and education, his ability to plan and design within proscribed financial boundaries a proven fact, and his relationship with the client a model of human behavior.

There are no rules and regulations that govern the "care and feeding" of clients nor any client rules for the "care and feeding" of designers. There are only the commonsense actions of people dealing with each other, and you will each of you bring to those dealings your own golden rules, polished bright or tarnished according to your own individual desires.

To be successful in your relationships, you must recognize the truth of what has often been repeated in this book—that this is a service, and must be so rendered. A client's complaint must be dealt with as quickly as possible; an error must be righted speedily. No telephone call should remain unanswered, no letter ignored. Problems must be faced the moment they arise. No trouble on a job really disappears when you try to kick it under your rug; the only thing you can lose that way is your reputation as a responsible planner and designer.

If everything you do is well done, that still doesn't mean an end to your organization problems. If you are good planners and good designers and are highly recommended to many clients, you must inevitably come face-to-face with a decision about the size of your operation. Do you keep your company small, retaining your own personal involvement in all phases of each job you handle, or do you expand, departmentalize, and administer the involvements of others? If the company you build is to be a big one, is it still to return its profits to one man, or do you share the wealth by spreading ownership, management, and profits among all who contribute to the company growth?

Again there is no one answer. There is instead the personal answer of the individual designer arrived at through the particular interplay of intellectual and philosophical attributes which enhance or abridge his life experience.

CHECKLIST L   PROJECT PROCEDURES

Below, in the logical order in which each should be accomplished, are the procedural steps to be followed in an office planning and design project. The items preceded by an asterisk (*) are those that would be used only on larger jobs.

As you get involved in an ever-increasing number of jobs that are being worked on concurrently, schedule following takes on greater importance. Therefore, in addition to using this list to make certain that nothing has been overlooked, you should use it in conjunction with your project schedule, in order to make certain that everything is done on time.

1. Interview—Operational Requirements (Checklist A).
*2. Interview—Departmental Questionnaire (Checklist B).

*Checklist L 185
Project
Procedures*

3. A tour of premises.
4. Inventory (Checklist C).
5. Establish space standards.
6. Tabulate footage (Checklist E).
7. Space study (Checklist G).
    Use latest, most detailed plan obtainable.
    Field check if possible.
    Obtain signed approval before continuing with design or working drawings.
*8. Evaluation report (Checklist F).
    This step may sometimes require a budget. If so, you may have to review the construction part of Checklist D—Design and Construction Requirements.
9. Work letter (Checklist H).
            or
    *Program for a new building.
10. Design meeting.
    Design and construction requirements (Checklist D). After this meeting the total project effort should be scheduled.
11. Budget.
12. Design.
13. Design and revised budget presentation (Checklist I).
    Obtain signed approval of budget.
14. Working drawings (Checklist J).
    Use latest, most detailed plans obtainable.
    Field check, if possible.
    Client should approve all drawings before they are sent out for bids.
15. Invite bids.
16. Approve bids.
17. Issue purchase orders.
18. Supervise construction.
19. Schedule move (Checklist K).
20. Punch list of items to be completed.

Almost every listed step requires client approval before you proceed to the next step, and every step must be reported to the client in detailed minutes. Any attempt to take shortcuts or eliminate any of the steps in your procedure can be an invitation to disaster through the creation of unnecessary problems.

TOMORROW

The first record of environmental benefits given to an employee dates back to the middle of the nineteenth century. "Bob, make up the fires, and buy another coal scuttle before you dot another i." Those were the words of Mr. Scrooge to Bob Cratchit, and they were prompted by the very effective labor arbitrators of those days, the ghosts of Christmas Past, Christmas Present, and Christmas Yet to Come.

Although employee benefits were long in coming and hard-won at first, the pace has quickened. The whole aspect of office and office procedure and office environment is changing—and changing quickly. So quickly, in fact, that before the word can be written, tomorrow becomes yesterday.

Tomorrow's space study will be the printout from taped information fed into a computer programmed for the particular physical characteristics of a specific floor in a specific building.

The working drawings will be gathered from an information retrieval system, and the renderings will stem from conceptual sketches done by a light pen on a cathode-ray tube.

The challenge of yesterday's effort was but a tranquil pursuit compared

Office Planning and Design

with the excitement of creative change that faces us. We do not know what the form and shape of tomorrow's business will be. We do not know what the practice of law will be like, or what role the accountant will play, or how the advertising agency will be organized. Will the law library be a microfilm reader? Will the accountant press a button to get an up-to-the-minute audit? How will the media department of an agency gather its information—and what will the media be?

The environeticist, designing the things people need and planning the places in which they use them, must face this wonderful challenge motivated, as he always has been, by a desire to build.

Man shows a tendency of late to tear down, simply because he is unsure of any goals toward which he can build. Even criticism has been destructive, and destruction without planned reconstruction and replacement is not the purpose of criticism and certainly not the purpose of creative effort. Those of us whose lives are to be devoted to planning and designing, must, in our critical thinking, think constructively or we shall not be planners at all.

Our planning, aimed as it must be to help the ennoblement of man, will perhaps someday allow us all to enjoy this 2-billion-man satellite of ours, as we continue to circle the sun in perpetual orbit.

ILLUSTRATIONS

DRAWINGS

		Page numbers
1.	Space standards—private office, 270 square feet	44
2.	Space standards—private office, 330 square feet	44
3.(a)-(h)	Space standards—work stations, furniture, and equipment	46, 48
4.	Floor measurement for single and divided tenancy	50
5.	Alternate building scheme No. 1	54
6.	Alternate building scheme No. 2	54
7.	Alternate building scheme No. 3	54
8.	Organization chart	66
9.	Area calculations	68
10.	Space study—rough	70
11.	Space study—rough	72
12.	Space study—rough	74
13.	Space study	76
14.(a)-(c)	Furniture plans—developmental	82
15.	Design presentation—design plan	92
16.	Design presentation—perspective rendering	94
17.	Design presentation—design board	96
18.	Furniture plan	98
19.	Working drawing—furniture, telephone, and electrical plan	100
20.	Working drawing—construction plan	102
21.	Working drawing—reflected ceiling plan	104
22.	Working drawing—paint and flooring plan	106
23.	Working drawing—elevations and details	108

Illustrations

PHOTOGRAPHS

All photographs are of installations planned and designed by Saphier, Lerner, Schindler, Inc. The names of the companies for whom these spaces were designed are listed below. Photographer credits are in parentheses.

1., 2., 3. Offices of ABC Corporation, D. L. O'Donoghue Corporation *(Andres Lander)*	132
4. Overfile storage, First National City Bank, Hubshman Factors Dept. *(Andres Lander)*	134
5. Overfile storage, Hiram Walker Inc. *(Louis Reens)*	134
6. Overfile work area, National Association of Manufacturers *(Marc Neuhoff)*	135
7. Overfile work area, National-Kinney *(Ben Schnall)*	135
8. Wall-hung storage, Saphier, Lerner, Schindler, Inc. *(Alexander Georges)*	136
9. Under-desk storage, Saphier, Lerner, Schindler, Inc. *(Alexander Georges)*	137
10., 11. Overfile projection room, Hooker Chemical Corporation *(Edward Ozern)*	138
12. Storage area as space divider *(Louis Reens)*	139
13., 14. Secretarial corridor *(Louis Reens)*	140
15., 16. Area control, National-Kinney *(Ben Schnall)*	141
17. Selling area, G. Schirmer, Inc. *(Louis Reens)*	142
18., 19., 20. Multiple purpose areas, National Credit Offices, Division of Dun & Bradstreet, Inc. *(Louis Reens)*	143
21., 22. Dual-purpose areas, L. Grief & Bros. *(Louis Reens)*	144
23., 24. Dual-purpose room, McCann-Erickson, Inc., Chicago *(Andres Lander)*	145
25., 26. Dual-purpose room, McCann Erickson, Inc., Chicago *(Andres Lander)*	146
27., 28. Dual-purpose room, Saphier, Lerner, Schindler, Inc. *(Louis Reens)*	147
29., 30. Dual-purpose room, Century Theatres, Inc. *(Marc Neuhoff)*	148
31., 32. Dual-purpose room, Saphier, Lerner, Schindler, Inc. *(Alexander Georges)*	149
33. Dual-purpose room, Witco Chemical Company, Inc. *(Jerry Darvin)*	150
34. Compact work area, Saphier, Lerner, Schindler, Inc. *(Alexander Georges)*	151
35., 36. Design details, Inland Credit Corporation *(Louis Reens)*	152
37., 38. Design details, Hooker Chemical Corporation *(Louis Reens)*	153
39. Design details, Witco Chemical Company, Inc. *(Jerry Darvin)*	154
40. Design details, Hooker Chemical Corporation *(Louis Reens)*	155
41. Design details, Combustion Engineering, Inc. *(Louis Reens)*	155

INDEX

Accounting department, 120, 172, 180–181
Air conditioning (see Heating, ventilating and air conditioning)
Architect, 163, 166
Authorization forms, change orders, 120, 121
   job, 120
   for purchasing, 107, 167

Bidding, 116–118, 167
   awards, 118
   forms for, 116
   instructions for, 116
   sealed, 116
Board rooms (see Conference rooms)
Budget, 17, 21–23, 59, 73–80, 167–169
   form of, 79
   as part of design presentation, 90, 97
Building, 119–123
   alternate schemes for, 52–56
   codes, 51, 112
   field changes, 120, 124
   schedule, 119
   single occupancy, 51–57
   standards, 36
      substituting for, 77
   supervision, 119–123, 125, 167, 169, 179
Building Owners and Managers Association, 47, 51

Cabinet details, 103, 105, 168, 169
   and elevations, 105, 114

Cabinet details, shop drawings for, 118
   for special facilities, 40
Ceilings, 37, 88
Checklists, 8
   departmental questionnaire (B), 33–34
   design and construction requirements (D), 36–40
   design presentation (I), 110
   evaluation report (F), 58–61
   inventory (C), 34–36
   the move (K), 126–129
   operational requirements (A), 23–33
   project procedures (L), 184
   space study (G), 86
   tabulation form (E), 57
   work letter (H), 87
   working drawings (J), 111
Conference rooms, 25, 27, 40
Construction requirements, checklist of, 36–40
Contract, 173–175
Contractor, general, 51, 116, 121, 125
   payments to, 118
   of record, 116
Controller, design company, 172, 180, 181
Costs (see Job cost analysis; Tenant extra costs)

Data processing room, 28
Departmental questionnaire, 13–16
   checklist B, 33–34
Design, 17–21, 80–86
   company, 166–184

191

Index

Design, company, files, 172, 176
　philosophy, 181–184
　procedure, 173–181
　　checklist L, 184
　coordinator, 171
　department, 171, 177, 178
　meeting, 17–21, 167, 168
　presentation, 83, 90–97, 168
　　board, 90, 91
　　checklist I, 110
　　perspective rendering, 90
　　plan, 90
　requirements for, checklist D, 36–40
Designer, 121, 166, 168
Dining areas, 25, 31
　for after hours, 32
Doors, bucks, and hardware, 37, 88, 113

Electrical equipment, 17, 32, 35, 37, 39, 88
　(*See also* Working drawings, furniture, telephone, and electrical plan *and* reflected ceiling plan)
Engineering, coordination of, 99, 101, 117, 118
　mechanical, 75, 99, 101, 103, 105
　structural, 75, 99, 101, 103
Estimating, 79, 169, 177
Estimator, 169, 177
Evaluation report, checklist F, 58–61
Executive area, 25, 26
Expediter, 110, 122, 171

Fees, 173–175
Field supervisor, 119–123, 169
Files and file room, 28
　(*See also* Job files)
Finishing trades, 77
Flexibility of layout, 32, 33, 107
Flooring, 37, 39, 88, 113
　(*See also* Paint and flooring plan)
Furniture and equipment, catalogs and samples, 169, 177
　delivery of, 121–123, 171
　details for, 40
　inventory of, checklist C, 34–36
　plan of, 17, 99, 101, 103, 112
　specifying and purchasing, 17, 39, 103, 107–110, 168, 169

Heating, ventilating, and air conditioning, 31, 32, 38, 75, 88, 103, 105
　for after hours, 31, 32

Identification numbers, 24, 34, 42, 65, 111, 112

Industrial designer, 162
Inspection of client premises, 12, 13
Interior decorator, 162
Interior designer, 162
Interviewing client personnel, 13–16
　(*See also* Departmental questionnaire)
Inventory, 13, 16, 17
　checklist C, 34–36
　simplified form, 67

Job cost analysis, 60, 180
Job files, 176, 177
Job numbers, 112, 176

Kitchens (*see* Dining areas)

Leases (*see* Work letter)
Library, 28

Mail and shipping rooms, 30, 38, 40
Measurements of floor areas, 47, 49, 69, 168
　factors, for gross building footage, 51
　for interdepartmental traffic, 45
　for intradepartmental traffic, 45
　of rentable vs. useable footage, 49
　for single or multiple occupancy floors, 49
Meeting rooms (*see* Conference rooms)
Minutes of meetings, 10–12, 176, 177
　interim review of, 16
Moving, 121–126, 167
　checklist K, 126–129
　committee, 123
Multiple occupancy floors, 51

Office Furniture Dealer, 161
Office Furniture Manufacturer, 161
Offices, private, 25, 26, 38
　semiprivate, 26
　special purposes, 27, 31
Open areas, 26, 32, 33
Operational requirements, 8–17
　checklist A, 23–33
　short form for, 65
Organization chart, 8, 9, 65, 69

Paint and flooring plan, 105, 113
　(*See also* Flooring)
Painting and wall covering, 88
Partitions, 37, 39, 87
Personnel, administration, design company, 171, 172
　client list of, 10

Personnel, design company list of, 166–172
　hiring of, 166
　production, design company, 167–171
Plans, architectural, 64
　core, 69, 176
　delivery dates for, 75
　electrical, 17, 99, 101, 112
　engineering, 75, 99, 101
　of existing space, 9
　field check of, 168
　furniture, 17
　rental, 49, 64, 175
　telephone, 17, 99, 101, 112
　transparencies of, 99, 176
　(See also Space study; Working drawings)
Plumbing, 32, 38, 88, 103
Project, coordinator, 170
　designer, 121, 168
　developer, 171
　director, 109, 120, 121, 171
　scheduling, 170, 179–181
Projection room, 28
Punch list, 125
Purchasing, authorization form for, 107, 167
　expediter, 110
　order for, 109
　program for, 17, 107–110

Real Estate Board, New York City, 49
Real estate consultant, 51, 73
Real estate manager, 51
Reception room, 24
Rentable footage, 47–51
Reports, 42–57
　evaluation, checklist F, 58–61
　interim review of, 16, 43, 57
Reproduction room, dark room, 30
Rest room, 31, 40

Sales rooms, 27, 40
Secretarial areas, 25, 26, 29
Shop drawings, 112, 117, 118, 167
Single occupancy, building, 51–57
　alternating schemes for, 52–57

Single occupancy, building, evaluating cost of, 51, 58–61
　evaluation report, checklist F, 58–61
　floors, 49
Space, analyst, 168
　standards, 42, 43
　study, 9, 64–73, 168, 175, 176
　checklist G, 86, 87
　department, 175, 176
Storage, closets, 32, 38, 39
　rooms, 30, 40
Supervision (see Building, supervision)

Tabulation, form, checklist E, 57
　short form for, 67
　of square feet, 42–45
Technical drafting, 120
　coordinator, 170
　department, 120, 169–171, 178, 179
Telephone, equipment for, 17, 35, 37, 40, 85, 88
　equipment room, 29, 119
　(See also Plans, telephone; Working drawings, furniture, telephone, and electrical plan)
Tenant extra costs, 77, 78, 116
Time slips, 176, 180
Toilets, private, 25, 31, 40

Useable footage, 45, 47, 49

Work letter, 22, 73–78, 176
　checklist H, 87, 88
　negotiating the, 73–78
Working drawings, 64, 99–107, 167, 169
　cabinet details, 103, 105, 114
　checklist J, 111–114
　construction plan, 103, 113
　elevations and details, 103, 105, 114
　furniture, telephone, and electrical plan, 17, 99, 112
　general notes for, 112
　paint and flooring plan, 105, 113
　reflected ceiling plan, 103, 113
　shop drawings, 112
　(See also Plans)